# First Steps in SAP® S/4HANA Sales and Distribution (SD)

John von Aspen

# Thank you for purchasing this book from Espresso Tutorials!

Like a cup of espresso coffee, Espresso Tutorials SAP books are concise and effective. We know that your time is valuable and we deliver information in a succinct and straightforward manner. It only takes our readers a short amount of time to consume SAP concepts. Our books are well recognized in the industry for leveraging tutorial-style instruction and videos to show you step by step how to successfully work with SAP.

Check out our YouTube channel to watch our videos at *https://www.youtube.com/user/EspressoTutorials*.

If you are interested in SAP Finance and Controlling, join us at *http://www.fico-forum.com/forum2/* to get your SAP questions answered and contribute to discussions.

## Related titles from Espresso Tutorials:

▶ Kevin Riddell, Rajen Iyver: Practical Guide to SAP® GTS, Part 1: SPL Screening and Compliance Management
*http://5100.espresso-tutorials.com*

▶ Kevin Riddell, Rajen Iyver: Practical Guide to SAP® GTS, Part 2: Preference and Customs Management
*http://5134.espresso-tutorials.com*

▶ Tobias Götz, Anette Götz: Practical Guide to SAP® Transportation Management (2nd edition)
*http://5082.espresso-tutorials.com*

▶ Kevin Riddell, Rajen Iyver: Practical Guide to SAP® GTS, Part 3: Bonded Warehouse, Foreign Trade Zone, and Duty Drawback
*http://5162.espresso-tutorials.com*

▶ Marjorie Wright: Credit Management in SAP® S/4HANA
*http://5300.espresso-tutorials.com*

John von Aspen
**First Steps in SAP® S/4HANA Sales and Distribution (SD)**

| **ISBN**: | 978-3-96012-859-5 |
| **Editor**: | Karen Schoch |
| **Cover Design**: | Philip Esch |
| **Cover Photo**: | istockphoto # 15939021 (c) Yuri |
| **Interior Book Design**: | Johann-Christian Hanke |

All rights reserved.

1st Edition 2020, Gleichen

© 2020 by Espresso Tutorials GmbH

URL: *www.espresso-tutorials.com*

**Feedback**
We greatly appreciate any feedback you may have concerning this book. Please send your feedback via email to: *info@espresso-tutorials.com*.

# Table of Contents

# Introduction

This is an important resource for anyone interested in learning about the Sales and Distribution (SD) module in SAP S/4HANA. The book is specifically tailored for people who wish to gain an understanding of the processes, functionality, and key features of SD—what it is, how it works, and where it fits in with the other modules of SAP S/4HANA. We'll take a journey with a new business user as she explores the system and gains new insight into using the Sales and Distribution module to meet her company's business needs.

Sales is a key function for every business and can be one of the most complex. Managing customers, taking orders, honoring agreements, generating customer-specific pricing, checking product availability, shipping, and billing are the heart and soul of SAP SD, and the primary drivers of success for many companies. SAP S/4HANA offers a great deal of flexibility in configuring these functions and now with embedded analytical reporting, it offers the tools to both analyze and respond to real-time data, and help companies drive towards process optimization.

I'd like to thank the following people without whom this book would not have been possible: Alice Adams for starting me on this adventure and seeing me through to the end, Karen Schoch for her editorial assistance, my wife Myuriel and daughter Lauren who give the love and support that makes it all worthwhile, and my mother who started me on the adventure of life and always encouraged me to write.

John von Aspen

We have added a few icons to highlight important information. These in-clude:

## Tips

Tips highlight information that provides more details about the subject being described and/or additional background information.

## Attention

Attention notices highlight information that you should be aware of when you go through the examples in this book on your own.

## Excercises

Exercises help you to solidify and deepen your knowledge.

Finally, a note concerning the copyright: all screenshots printed in this book are the copyright of SAP SE. All rights are reserved by SAP SE. Copyright pertains to all SAP images in this publication. For the sake of simplicity, we do not mention this specifically underneath every screenshot.

# 1 The Sales and Distribution module

**This chapter introduces the SAP Sales and Distribution module. We discuss what it is and how it fits in with the overall SAP solution.**

One of the things you notice early on in the SAP world is that there are AAP (acronyms-a-plenty). This is not surprising coming from a company with an acronym for a name. Yes, 'SAP' is an acronym for the rather complicated German phrase 'Systeme, Anwendugen und Produkte in Der Datenverarbeitung' (don't worry, it won't be on the test). It is clearly not a company founded by marketing folks. However, when it comes to making ERP (enterprise resource planning) software—see, another acronym—there are few equals. This brings us to the acronym that we discuss in this chapter, 'SD'. As you may have already deduced from the chapter heading, this stands for Sales and Distribution. So what is it? And how does it relate to other acronym-labelled modules such as MM, PP, FI, PM, and...OMG (LOL)? And what the heck is a module anyway? Well, dear reader, you've come to the right place because in this book we delve into this, and other mysteries, surrounding the most important module in SAP!

## 1.1 Modules and more

So let's get started, beginning with the term *module*. What is a module in SAP exactly? A module is a grouping of like functionality. Because SAP software is famously a mile wide and a mile deep, it can do all kinds of things; everything from purchasing to accounting, and production planning to human resources. As a way to organize features and functionalities, SAP has the concept of modules, which, as we said, is a grouping of like functionality. The most typically used modules, also sometimes called the 'core' modules, are SD (yay!), Materials Management (MM), and Finance and Controlling (FICO). Note that we also used to include PP (Production Planning) in this illustrious group, but with the global changes in manufacturing, it's just not as common as it used to be; I'm just going to have to 'Pluto-ize' it and remove it from our core solar system. Circling around this core solar system are many other modules such as Customer Service, Plant Maintenance, Human Resources, Asset Management, Global Trade Services, etc. etc. etc. One of the nice things about SAP is that even though all that functionality is in the software, you can choose to use as much or as little of it as you want. The same thing holds true within any given module.

For example, within the Sales and Distribution module, there is a lot of functionality available, but you can choose to use as much or as little of it as your company needs. For example, there is a core set of functionality around Sales Orders, Deliveries, and Billing documents, but there are also all kinds of other document categories such as Quotations, Contracts, Inquiries, and plenty more that you can use, or not use, depending on what makes sense for your company and industry. More on this later.

---

**ERP**

 Enterprise resource planning (ERP) is a category of software for which SAP is famous. It is essentially software that helps companies run their business and includes a wide variety of functionality—from Purchasing to Sales, and Production to Finance, and everything in between. The ERP terminology grew out of an earlier software category called MRP (materials resource planning), which was all about controlling/matching supply and demand. Just to confuse things, ERP is also an SAP release name. You may hear the term 'ERP Core' which is a way of distinguishing the core SAP system from add-on products that came later, such as Supplier Relationship Management (SRM), Customer Relationship Management (CRM), Advanced Planning and Optimization (APO), and so on. The core SAP system is also referred to as ECC (Enterprise Core Component). Whew, told you there were a lot of acronyms!

---

## 1.2 Sales and Distribution, I presume?

The Sales and Distribution module encompasses the features and functions that enable a business to sell, ship, and bill for their products and services. At the center of the SD Universe is the *sales order*, which is the central document of the sales process (makes sense, right?). The sales order is where we record the details of a sales transaction—what was sold, who it was sold to, how much it was sold for, and when it can be delivered. The sales order is the central repository of the who, what, when, where, and how of an individual sale. After we have a sales order and we're ready to ship, we then move on to the *delivery document*. This is where we handle the *logistics execution* of what was sold; i.e., the details of moving products from our warehouse out to the customer. In the delivery document, you find information such as the customer ship-to address, the materials, the quantities, warehouse picking, and packing details. Logistics execution makes up the 'D' part of SD and is tightly integrated with the order-to-cash process.

Once we've shipped the goods to the customer, it's time for them to pay for our fabulous products. This is where billing comes in. The billing document records things such as: who should be billed, what should be billed, the price, the quantities, and how we're going to get paid. All the document types that I've mentioned so far (sales order, delivery, billing) are electronic documents in the SAP system. All of them can also be accompanied by a printed document that SAP refers to as *output*. For example, an SAP billing document can also generate a printed billing document output if you need to send an invoice to your customer. Output can also be in an electronic format if you need to generate an email or EDI document.

## OTC and more TLAs

 Another way of describing the SAP modules is by business process work stream. We love our TLAs (three letter acronyms) and for the SD area, it's all about OTC (order-to-cash). Other acronyms you'll often come across are P2P (procure to pay) for MM (materials management), and R2R (record to report) for FICO. Looks like those latter acronyms had to make do with a '2' instead of a 'to'. Guess there can only be one king!

At the core of the Sales and Distribution module is a simple process: sales order to delivery to billing document. However, like life, there can be plenty of variations and deviations along this simple path. Many things can happen before, during, and after, in order to support a huge variety of business flows. Additionally, for each and every step along the way, there is also a rich feature set of functionality—pricing, texts, and partners, to name just a few. Because SAP is a 'software package' (not custom built for just one company) it has to be able to handle a million and one different scenarios and business requirements without having to write custom code. And that's why configuration is such a beautiful thing! Configuration allows us to set up all of these flows and support a multitude of business requirements by making settings in the software—but more on that later.

Once we've billed an order, how do we get to the 'cash' part of the order-to-cash process? That's where our friends in finance come in. After we've billed, we need to let accounting know that we've completed the sale and that it's time to collect payment. Of course, all this is automated in SAP. The billing document automatically triggers the creation of a corresponding *ac-*

*counting document* in the Finance (FI) module. The accounting document records the sale as revenue and posts an offsetting entry on the customer's account. Finally, on the accounts receivable side, the customer's payment (the 'cash') gets applied to the open receivable, thereby clearing it and closing the loop. Simple, right? Well, it depends. Sometimes it is, and sometimes there can be all kinds of variations and business rules which add complexity. But at its core, the SD process is pretty straightforward: sell it, ship it, and bill it!

## OTC and SD

 There's something a little funny about the terms 'order-to-cash' and 'sales and distribution'. In terms of people and process, our work stream is really more like 'order-to-billing', or even 'quotation-to-billing'. When a billing document is created (in the SD module), a corresponding accounting document is created (in the FI module), which posts to the customer's accounts receivable and general ledger accounts. At that point, we SD folks consider that it has passed over into the accounting world. We don't get involved with the 'cash' bit—that's for the bean counters!

By now you should have a general sense of what SD is about. So, let's buckle up our seat belts as we venture along the road to actually using it.

In Chapter 2, we'll embark on our journey by following the experience of our friend Lauren as she starts work at a new company and tries to make sense of SAP SD.

## SAP S/4HANA

 SAP S/4HANA is the latest incarnation of SAP's core enterprise software; a re-architected solution that runs very fast and uses an in-memory database instead of a traditional disc-based database. It moves the reporting and analytics into the same transactional system, instead of an external business data warehouse. SAP S/4HANA also comes with Fiori, the latest and greatest SAP user interface, accessible via a web browser. It's interesting to note that the number of the SAP S/4HANA release (e.g., 1809), represents the year (20**18**) and Quarter (**09**—September) of the release.

# 2 Training time

**Lauren was a little nervous as she began her second day at Brand X Industries. Her new boss, Carl, seemed nice enough, but her anxiety grew during the day as he took her around to meet the other department heads. He kept introducing her as a 'star' and saying how she was going help get things under control with the new SAP system. She really hoped she wouldn't disappoint him.**

Lauren had spent a few hours the night before, and that morning, going through the SAP training manuals for Brand X. What she read seemed to make sense. There were sales orders and invoices, customers and materials—all things that she could relate to from her previous experience as a senior customer service representative at Oakbox Co. But there were also things that didn't make sense to her, such as 'condition records', 'document flow', 'output', and a lot of other unfamiliar SAP terms. In addition, she had no idea how it all fit together. Additionally, this was a new company for her, with new people, new processes, and to top it all off, a new industry!

Lauren breathed deeply and told herself to be patient. She knew that she learned best by actually getting her hands on a system and 'doing'. That's why she had asked to sit with one of the customer service reps that day to watch them work and help enter some orders.

## 2.1    Order in the court

Vanessa Roberts, a senior customer service representative for Brand X, greeted Lauren as she pulled up a chair to join Vanessa at her work cubicle. "These are the orders we received yesterday that I haven't entered in the system yet," said Vanessa, pointing to a stack of papers.

"Normally, I'd have these finished, but ever since we've gotten SAP we're struggling to catch up," she continued.

"Ok, well, I'm just going to watch what you do, and then hopefully be able to help a little bit," said Lauren, logging on to her new company laptop.

She opened her web browser and pasted in the URL for the SAP system from her training manual. She entered her user ID and password, and logged on (see Figure 2.1).

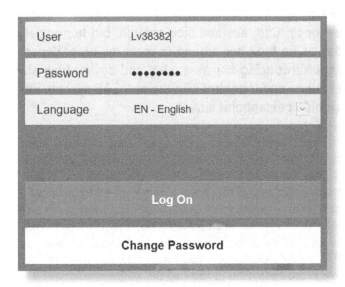

*Figure 2.1: Fiori logon screen*

Once she was logged on, she saw the screen shown in Figure 2.2.

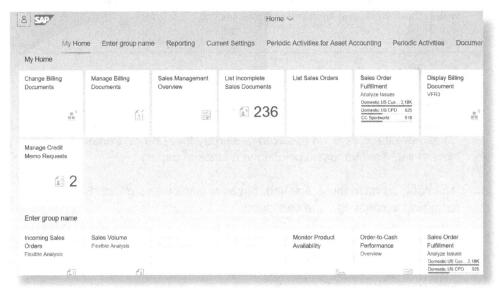

*Figure 2.2: Fiori Launchpad*

She knew from her training materials that this was the 'launchpad' and that each one of these square 'tiles' would allow her to do different things in the system. What she wanted to do now was to help Vanessa enter sales orders, but she initially couldn't see anything representing that on her screen. She scrolled down further and found the tile that she wanted (see Figure 2.3).

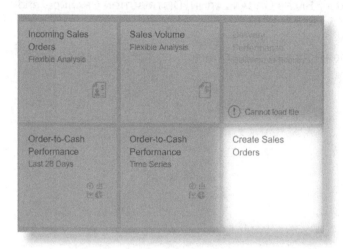

*Figure 2.3: Create Sales Orders tile*

She clicked on the CREATE SALES ORDERS tile and up popped the CREATE SALES DOCUMENT screen (see Figure 2.4).

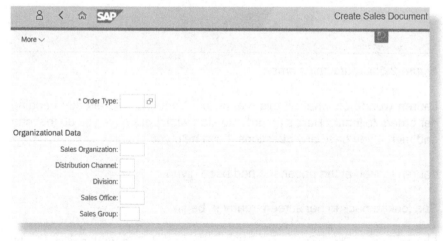

*Figure 2.4: Create Sales Document screen*

Ok, that wasn't too hard, she thought. But what's all this stuff here?...OR-
DER TYPE, SALES ORGANIZATION, DISTRIBUTION CHANNEL....what should
she put in those fields?

Vanessa saw the puzzled look on Lauren's face and explained, "We're
going to be putting in regular orders, which is code *ZOR*. Then, we always
put in *1710, 10, 00* for SALES ORGANIZATION, DISTRIBUTION CHANNEL, and
DIVISION, because we're in the US."

Lauren entered the information, as instructed, on her screen (see Figure
2.5).

*Figure 2.5: Create sales order*

Lauren wondered what all this meant, but Vanessa was already handing
her orders to input. "Here's an order to start with. Let's have you do that one
and then if you have any questions, I can help you."

Lauren looked at the paper she had been given.

She looked back to her screen, ready to begin.

She clicked on the screen, and nothing happened. She double clicked, still
nothing. She didn't see any icons or buttons that looked promising.

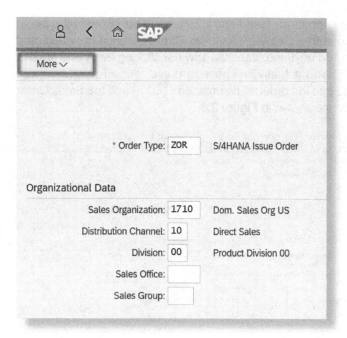

*Figure 2.6: Create sales order*

The only thing that looked remotely helpful was the MORE menu button (see Figure 2.6), so she clicked on it.

*Figure 2.7: Create sales order*

A dropdown menu appeared (see Figure 2.7), and she followed the menu path SALES DOCUMENT • CREATE. However, CREATE was in gray text, and clicking on it didn't do anything. Vanessa saw her clicking away and smiled. "Yeah, lovely SAP. You actually just have to press ⌑Enter⌑ (or CONTINUE) and that takes you into the order." She pressed ⌑Enter⌑ and the Sales Order screen popped up, as shown in Figure 2.8.

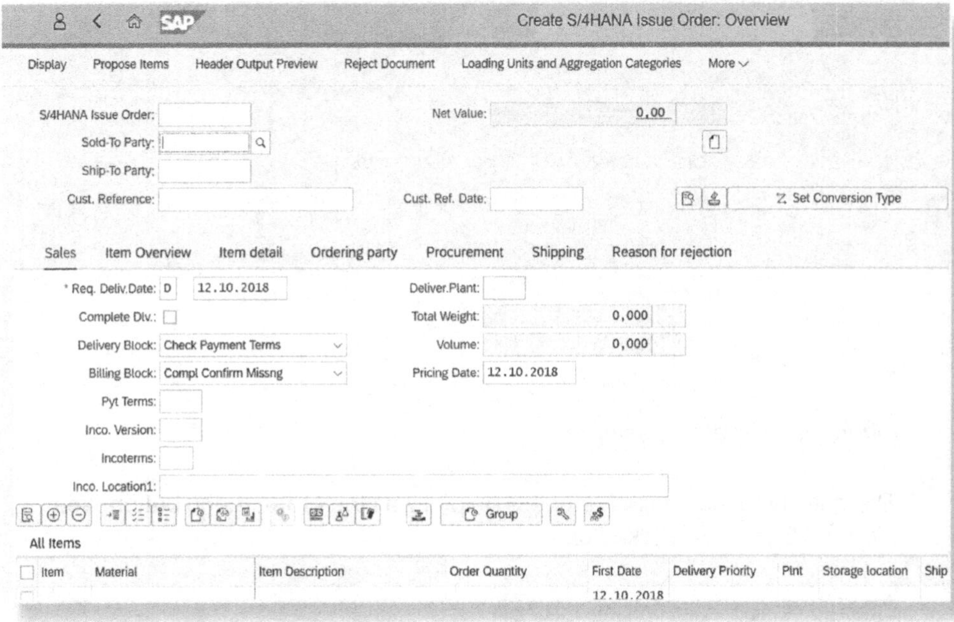

*Figure 2.8: Create sales order*

Whoa, there is a lot going on here, thought Lauren. Look at all those fields and buttons. She could feel her pulse quicken. She didn't want to appear clueless to Vanessa. She looked back at the paper order form she had in front of her.

The customer name was at the top of the form, so that seemed like a good place to start. She looked back at the SAP screen scanning for a 'Customer' field.

Vanessa could see Lauren's hesitation and said, "How about I enter this one for you first?"

"Ok, I think that will help," replied Lauren.

"Ok, the customer's name is Fast Bikes, so we go over here to the SOLD-TO PARTY field and look up their number", explained Vanessa (see Figure 2.9).

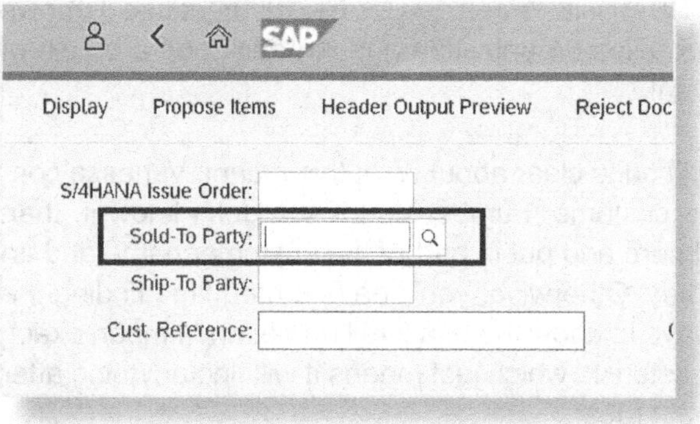

*Figure 2.9: Sold-To Party field*

"We do that by clicking on the little magnifying glass, and then the search screen pops up" (see Figure 2.10).

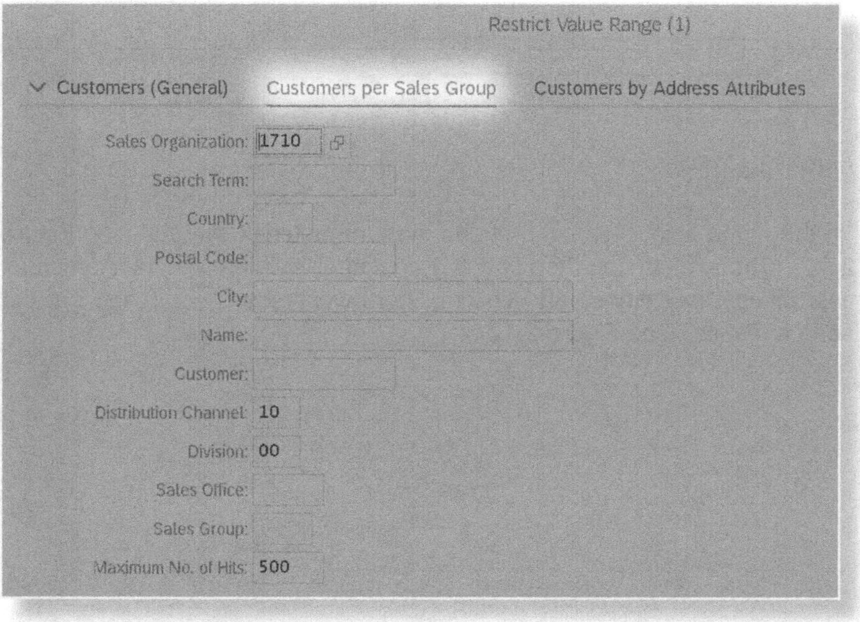

*Figure 2.10: Customer search screen*

"The heading at the top tells us which search we are using. In this case, we are searching for CUSTOMERS PER SALES GROUP," Vanessa clarified. "The screenshot shows that there are some other choices along the top as well, such as CUSTOMERS (GENERAL) and CUSTOMERS BY ADDRESS ATTRIBUTES. Basically, the choices just give us different fields to use when searching for

19

a customer. I like to use CUSTOMERS PER SALES GROUP because it shows only the customers in our sales organization and we don't see a bunch of other stuff that isn't relevant."

Lauren nodded, but wasn't quite clear about what this meant. Vanessa continued, "So, we need the customer number and if you don't know it, then you go to this name field here and put in part of the customer name and an asterisk. The asterisk is key. Otherwise, you'll have a hard time finding the customer because you have to know the exact full name, and I mean exact. It's just easier to use the asterisk, which just means it will find anything after it. Look, I'll show you what I mean."

Sales Organization: 1710

Search Term:

Country:

Postal Code:

City:

Name: fast*

Customer:

*Figure 2.11: Customer Search*

"In the name field, I type in *fast* and then the asterisk symbol" (see Figure 2.11)." The system can then find any customer starting with 'fast', such as 'fast bikes', 'fast times', and so on. Then, we press ⌈Enter⌉ and get the search results" (see Figure 2.12).

Restrict Value Range (1)                                                    ✕

> Customers (General)     Customers per Sales Group     Customers by Address Attributes     ...

| SOrg. | SearchTerm | Cty | PostalCode | City | Name 1 | Customer | DChl |
|-------|-----------|-----|-----------|------|--------|----------|------|
| 1710 | CBK01 | US | 10035 | NEW YORK | FAST BIKES INC.. | USCUST01-L | 10 |

1 Entry found

*Figure 2.12: Customer search tab*

"It only found one customer, Fast Bikes Inc., so that means there's only one that starts with 'fast'. That's the one we want, so we just double click on it and it brings the customer number into the SOLD-TO PARTY field" (see Figure 2.13).

*Figure 2.13: Sold-To Party field*

"So there it is. If we press ⌞Enter⌟, it also fills out the SHIP-TO PARTY field" (see Figure 2.14).

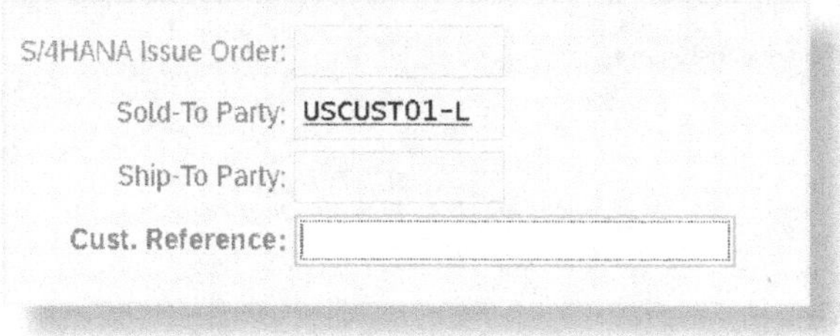

*Figure 2.14: Customer reference field*

"Oops, my mistake. It asks us first for the PO. This is where we put in the customer's PO number. SAP calls it CUST. REFERENCE, meaning that it's our customer's reference number for the order they are placing with us. Normally, that's the customer's purchase order. Their purchase order equals our sales order, right? They're buying from us with their purchase order and we are selling to them with our sales order".

"So", Vanessa explained, "we enter the customer's PO, and then it fills out the number in the SHIP-TO PARTY field" (see Figure 2.15).

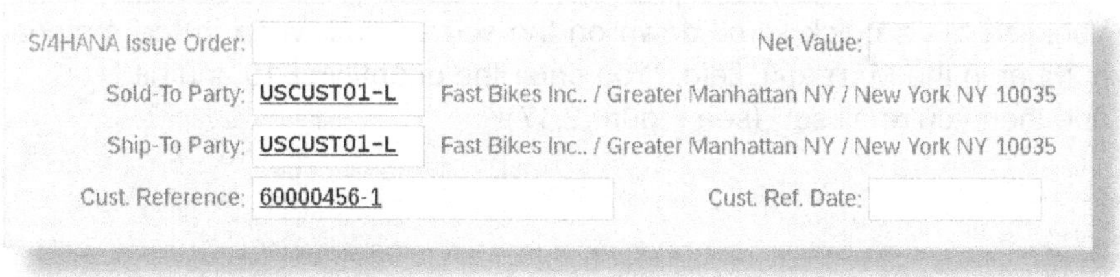

*Figure 2.15: Customer data*

"See? There's the address, in New York, and there's the Customer PO number I put in. Got it?"

Lauren nodded. That seemed pretty straightforward.

Vanessa continued, "So now we want to put in the materials. On this PO the customer wants 10 of our bike glasses, material MZ-FG-R200. You just scroll down the order and enter the material here in the line items section" (see Figure 2.16).

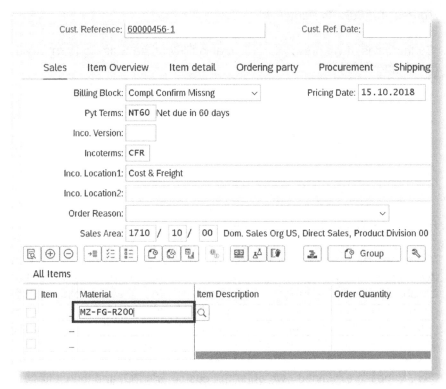

*Figure 2.16: Sales order line item—Material entry*

Vanessa did a quick scroll down on the screen and typed in the material number in the MATERIAL field. "You enter the quantity of 10 and hit [Enter], and then you're all set" (see Figure 2.17).

| | Item | Material | Item Description | Order Quantity | First Date | Delivery Priority | Plnt | Storage location | Ship./Re... |
|---|---|---|---|---|---|---|---|---|---|
| | 10 | MZ-FG-R200 | R200 Bike | 10 | 15.10.20... | 1 | 1710 | 171A | 1710 |
| | — | | | | 15.10.20... | | | | |

*Figure 2.17: Line item*

Lauren saw that a description for the material had appeared, as well as lots of other information. She also saw that there were spaces for other lines, where she guessed more materials could be entered.

"Now, you just click on the SAVE button at the bottom right, and your order is saved. It also tells you if anything's missing. The system then tells you your order number. This one is 32131." Lauren saw at the bottom left of the screen that a little message had popped up (see Figure 2.18).

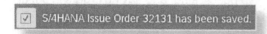

*Figure 2.18: Order saved*

"You can then choose DISPLAY or CHANGE (depending on which mode you are in) and look at the order you just created" (see Figure 2.19).

| | | | | | |
|---|---|---|---|---|---|
| 8 < ⌂ **SAP** | | Change S/4HANA Issue Order 32131: Overview | | | |

| Display | Display Document Flow | Status Overview | Propose Items | Header Output Preview | Reject Document | Loading Units and Aggregation Categories |

S/4HANA Issue Order: 32131     Net Value:    39,770,00 USD
Sold-To Party: USCUST01-L   Fast Bikes Inc.. / Greater Manhattan NY / New York NY 10035
Ship-To Party: USCUST01-L   Fast Bikes Inc.. / Greater Manhattan NY / New York NY 10035
Cust. Reference: 60000456-1    Cust. Ref. Date:     Ƶ Base Values

| Sales | Item Overview | Item detail | Ordering party | Procurement | Shipping | Reason for rejection |

* Req. Deliv.Date: D   15.10.2018     Deliver.Plant:
Complete Dlv.: ☐     Total Weight:    68,500 KG
Delivery Block: Check Payment Terms ⌄    Volume:    0,000
Billing Block: Compl Confirm Missng ⌄    Pricing Date: 15.10.2018
Pyt Terms: NT60   Net due in 60 days
Inco. Version:
Incoterms: CFR
Inco. Location1: Cost & Freight

All Items

| | Item | Material | Item Description | Order Quantity | First Date | Delivery Priority | Plnt | Storage location | Ship./Re... |
|---|---|---|---|---|---|---|---|---|---|
| ☐ | 10 | MZ-FG-R200 | R200 Bike | 10 | 15.10.20.. | 1 | 1710 | 171A | 1710 |

*Figure 2.19: Sales order change screen*

"And there it is," Vanessa concluded.

Yes, there it is, Lauren thought to herself. But what was all this other stuff on the screen? NET VALUE, DELIVERY BLOCK, and TOTAL WEIGHT? Where did that come from?

Vanessa grabbed a stack of orders and passed them to Lauren. "As many of these as you can get in would be great. Let's meet up again around 3 pm to see where we are, ok?"

## 2.2 The results

When they got back together that afternoon, Vanessa was flying through SAP screens on her computer—typing, clicking, and saving orders in a blur. "How many did you get through?" asked Vanessa.

"Only ten," replied Lauren, "it took a lot longer than I thought."

"That's ok, it's only your first time with SAP right? Anyway, anything is a help, and this is kind of like on-the-job training. So let's take a look."

Lauren started shuffling her papers to give Vanessa her order numbers but Vanessa was already typing away on her keyboard. "Ok, I see your orders here", Vanessa said (see Figure 2.20).

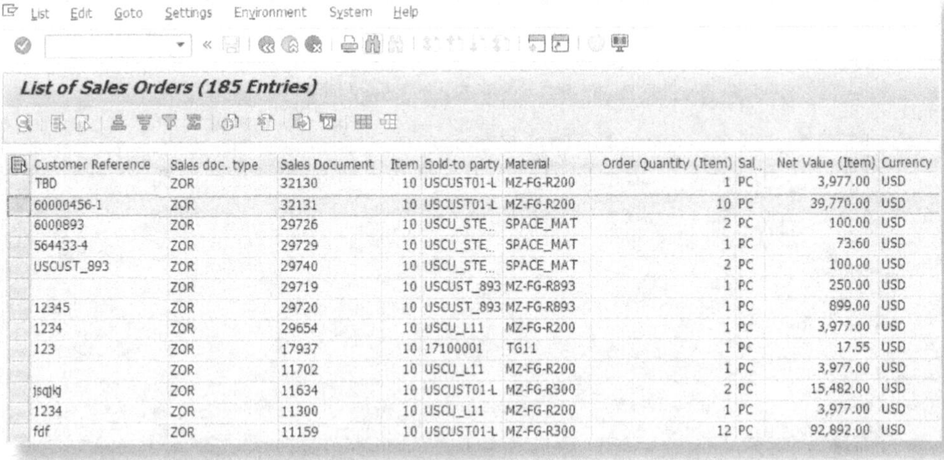

List Edit Goto Settings Environment System Help

### List of Sales Orders (185 Entries)

| Customer Reference | Sales doc. type | Sales Document | Item | Sold-to party | Material | Order Quantity (Item) | Sal_ | Net Value (Item) | Currency |
|---|---|---|---|---|---|---|---|---|---|
| TBD | ZOR | 32130 | 10 | USCUST01-L | MZ-FG-R200 | 1 PC | | 3,977.00 | USD |
| 60000456-1 | ZOR | 32131 | 10 | USCUST01-L | MZ-FG-R200 | 10 PC | | 39,770.00 | USD |
| 6000893 | ZOR | 29726 | 10 | USCU_STE_ | SPACE_MAT | 2 PC | | 100.00 | USD |
| 564433-4 | ZOR | 29729 | 10 | USCU_STE_ | SPACE_MAT | 1 PC | | 73.60 | USD |
| USCUST_893 | ZOR | 29740 | 10 | USCU_STE_ | SPACE_MAT | 2 PC | | 100.00 | USD |
| | ZOR | 29719 | 10 | USCUST_893 | MZ-FG-R893 | 1 PC | | 250.00 | USD |
| 12345 | ZOR | 29720 | 10 | USCUST_893 | MZ-FG-R893 | 1 PC | | 899.00 | USD |
| 1234 | ZOR | 29654 | 10 | USCU_L11 | MZ-FG-R200 | 1 PC | | 3,977.00 | USD |
| 123 | ZOR | 17937 | 10 | 17100001 | TG11 | 1 PC | | 17.55 | USD |
| | ZOR | 11702 | 10 | USCU_L11 | MZ-FG-R200 | 1 PC | | 3,977.00 | USD |
| jsqkj | ZOR | 11634 | 10 | USCUST01-L | MZ-FG-R300 | 2 PC | | 15,482.00 | USD |
| 1234 | ZOR | 11300 | 10 | USCU_L11 | MZ-FG-R200 | 1 PC | | 3,977.00 | USD |
| fdf | ZOR | 11159 | 10 | USCUST01-L | MZ-FG-R300 | 12 PC | | 92,892.00 | USD |

*Figure 2.20: List of Sales Orders screen*

She clicked on one of the orders from her list and it appeared on the screen (see Figure 2.21).

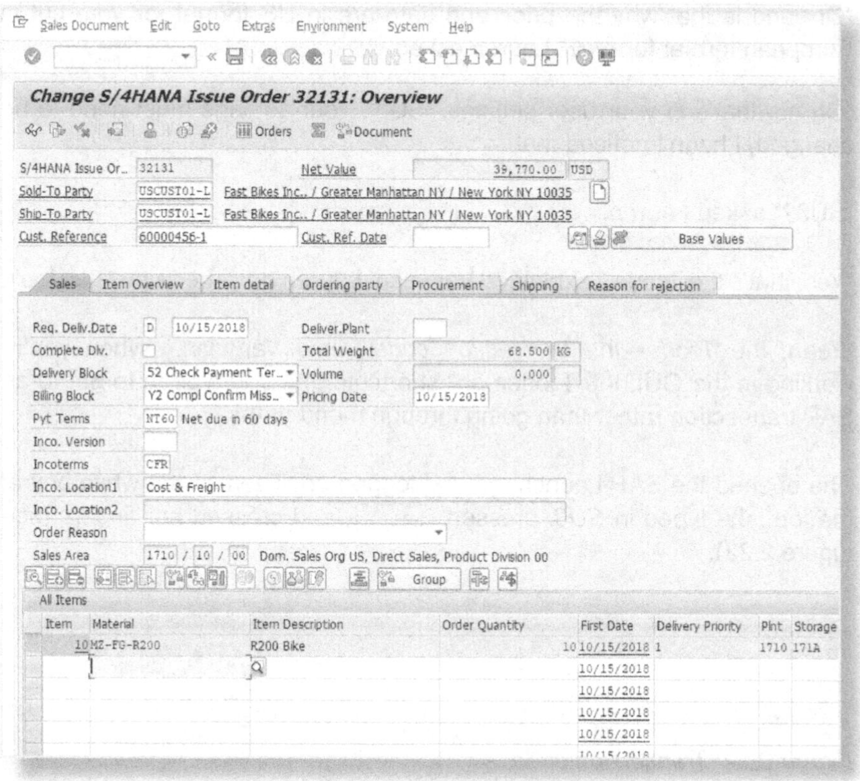

*Figure 2.21: Sales order—Change GUI*

"Ah, this is the one we did together," Vanessa pointed out.

"Hang on," said Lauren, "why does your screen look different?"

"Oh, I prefer using the gooey, it's just faster for order entry," Vanessa replied.

"Gooey?" Lauren was puzzled.

Vanessa spelled it out, "*G-U-I*...the consultants said it stood for *graphical user interface*. I know, nerd alert, right? It's the screen you get when you use the SAP LOGON icon instead of the web browser. It's just a different window into the SAP system, so it doesn't matter whether you come in from the web page like you did, or this way. It's all the same data. I find using the GUI faster for data entry, but the web is prettier and has everything on one start screen, so many people prefer that."

"Oh, and is that why the price and date are in US format for you, but in European format for me?" Lauren asked.

"Oh no, that's in your user settings, 'SU3'. Your settings must need to be changed, I hadn't noticed that."

"SU3?" asked Lauren.

"Yes, that's the Tcode," explained Vanessa. Lauren gave her a puzzled look.

"Yeah, the *Tcode*—the *transaction code*," said Vanessa. "When you're working in the GUI, the Tcodes are shortcuts that you type in to get to an SAP transaction rather than going through menu paths."

She opened the SAP Launchpad and logged on. Then, in the white box at the top, she typed in *SU3*, pressed Enter, and crossed her fingers (see Figure 2.22).

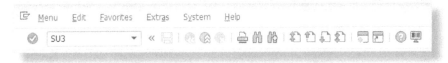

*Figure 2.22: Transaction code*

A screen popped up, showing her user id info (see Figure 2.23).

On the DEFAULTS tab, she saw that she could set the DECIMAL NOTATION, DATE FORMAT, and many other things.

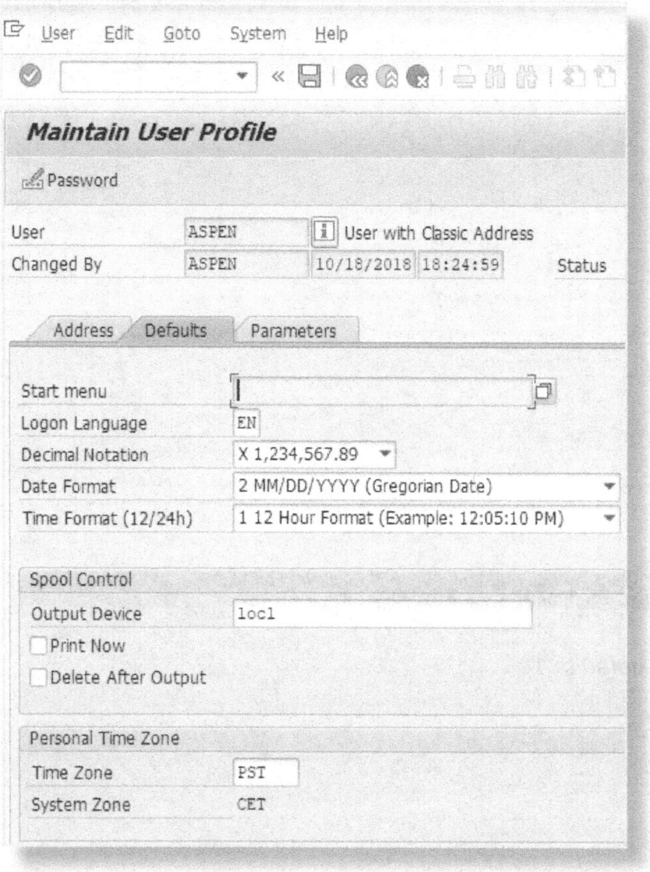

*Figure 2.23: User profile*

"Yep, you got it," said Vanessa, smiling. "You can also do the same thing in Fiori. You can set your user defaults there too, so you don't have to keep entering in the same things over and over. There's an icon that looks like a little person, and under that, there's a gear icon, where you can put your preference for time and date format, and also your defaults for sales organization" (see Figure 2.24).

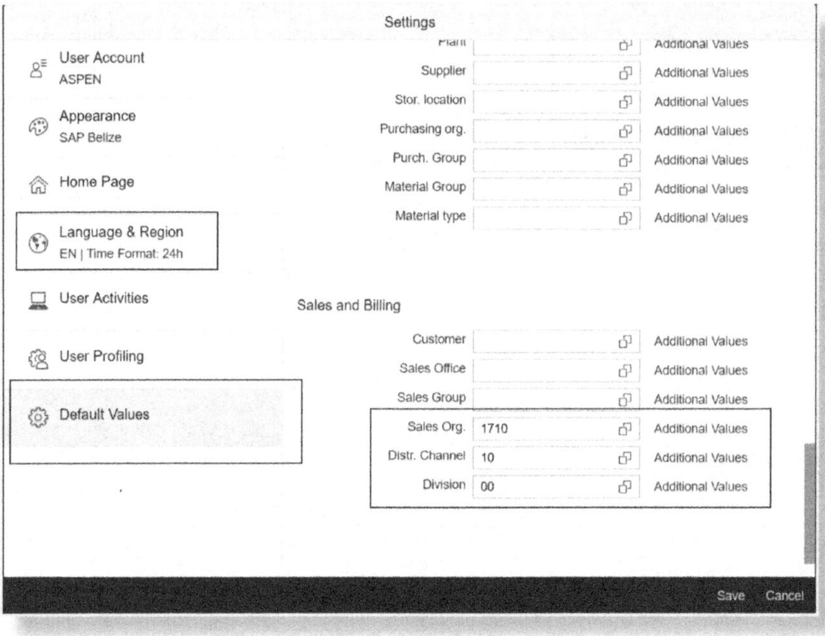

Figure 2.24: Fiori defaults 1

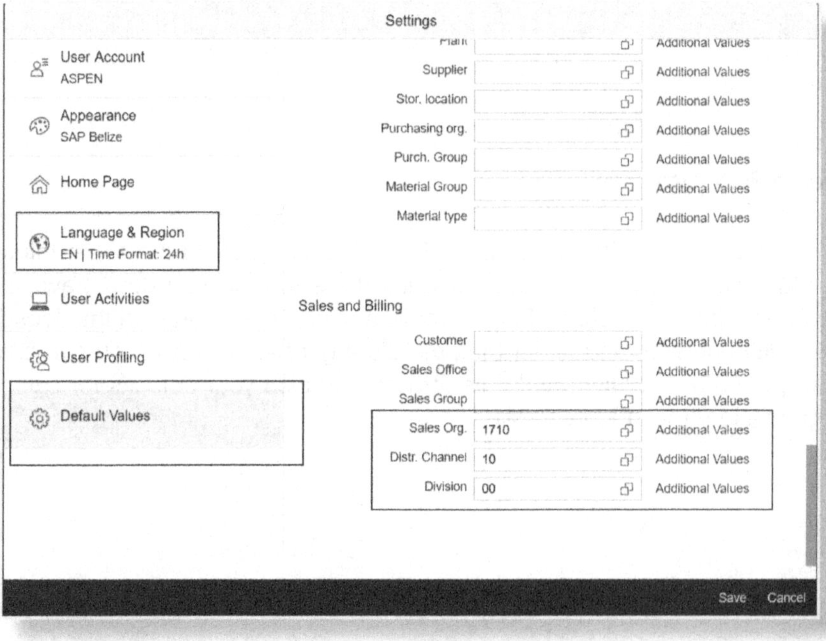

Figure 2.25: Fiori defaults

"Just out of curiosity, where do you see which orders were mine versus someone else's?", Lauren queried.

"Ooooh, your name is on everything you touch in SAP. That's one of the great things about it. There's no more denial about who did what. Your name gets stamped all over everything!", explained Vanessa. "If we go to the header of that sales order," she continued, "you can see the CREATED BY field right here on the SALES tab" (see Figure 2.26).

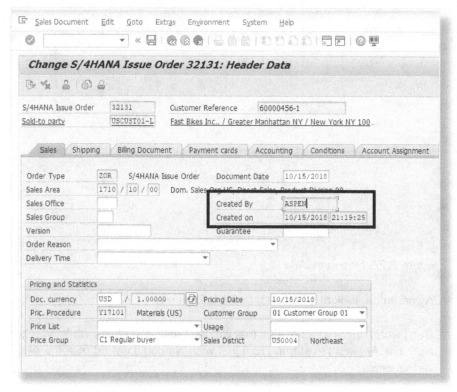

*Figure 2.26: Created By field*

"There's your user name, and the date and time."

"Whoa," exclaimed Lauren, "what are all these other tabs?"

"Oh yeah," said Vanessa. "SAP loves tabs. Tons of stuff there. And that's just the header. If we go to the line item level, there's even more."

A couple of fast clicks and they were looking at a whole new set of screens and tabs (see Figure 2.27).

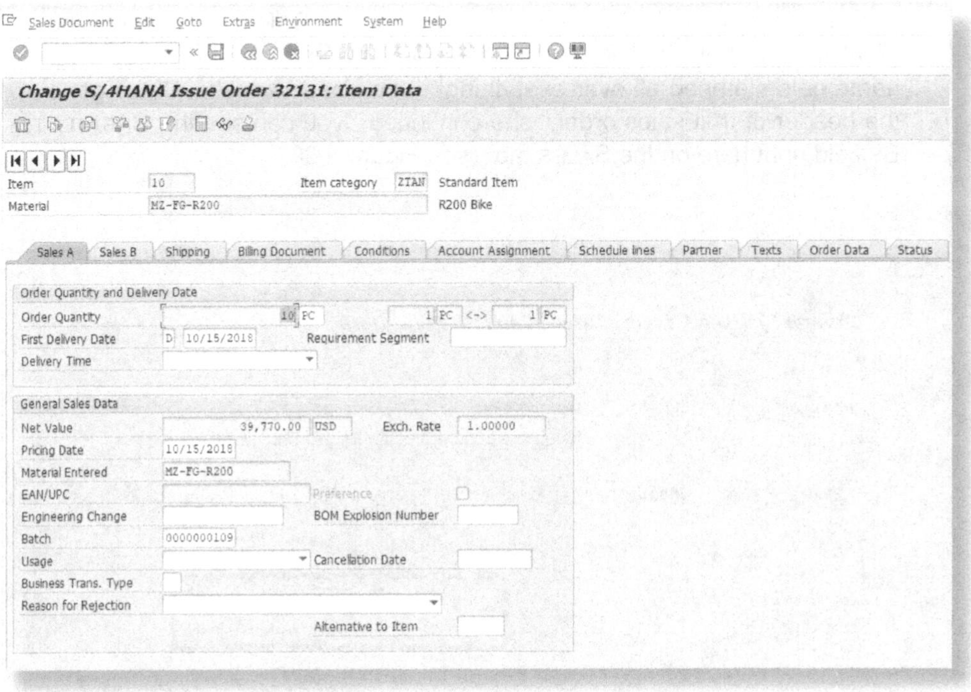

*Figure 2.27: Line item data*

"Ay caramba, look at all those tabs!" cried Lauren.

"Don't worry, there's lots of stuff that we don't use, and after a while, you get used to it. At least I'm starting to. I just wish we could get rid of some of it," said Vanessa.

"Hang on a sec, Vanessa. What exactly do you mean by 'header' and 'line item data'?"

"Look at this first sales order screen" (see Figure 2.28). "You can see some header data at the top, and some line item data at the bottom."

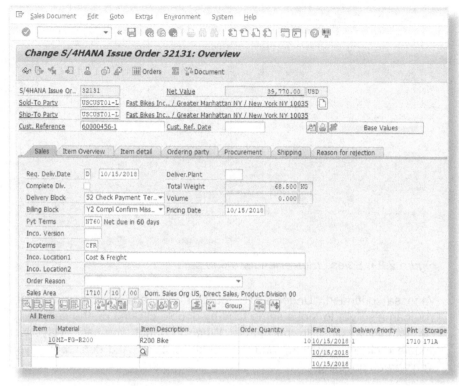

*Figure 2.28: Sales order screen*

"Hmm, so is this screen header data or line item data?" asked Lauren.

"Well, this screen shows a little of both. Kind of like an overview of everything".

Lauren stared at the screen.

"So, imagine you're buying stuff on Amazon" asked Vanessa. "You place an order, and all the details about you, your name, address, and credit card info, is the header information. And then, whatever you put in your cart is the line item data. So right now we just have our R200 BIKE glasses model in our cart, but we could order more things, and then we'd have more line items. And then each line item has a quantity, a price, and a date when it can ship, right? Well, it's just like that in SAP, except, of course, there can be a lot more information. If you ever want to move around in the order, you just go to the top menu path called GOTO and navigate from there" (see Figure 2.29).

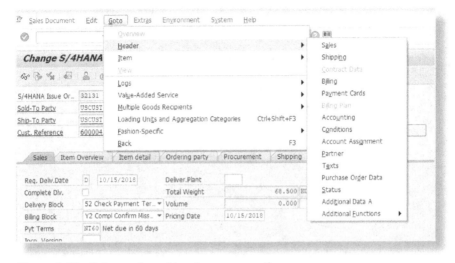

*Figure 2.29: Sales order—Header menu path*

Vanessa continued, "Under GOTO you can go to any header or item tab. You can also get to those same tabs by double-clicking on the item or on the magnifying glass in the header. When in doubt, you can always just double click on something and see what happens. And don't worry, you won't break anything."

"Do you mind if we stop for now? I've got to get these other orders in before 5 pm," asked Vanessa.

Lauren didn't mind. In fact, she was ready to call it a day. So many screens and fields, and so much information coming at her. She needed a little quiet time to digest it all.

## Benvenuto a Fiori!

The Fiori user interface is more than just a new look for SAP screens. Many of the standard delivered tiles are 'mashups' of multiple transactions, delivering more functionality in a single place. Rather than having to navigate to two different screens, a Fiori app can deliver the same information on one screen, with one click. Some of the apps even show simplified information on the tile itself—for example, the number of incomplete sales documents—so you don't even have to click at all!

# 3  The sales order

**In this chapter, we introduce sales orders, document types, and the SD Enterprise structure.**

Early the next day, Lauren decided that the Brand X SAP training manuals would be a good place to start. She had seen a lot yesterday, and while some of it made sense, there was still a lot that didn't. She decided she would create a sales order on her own and then reference the training manual when she had questions. Luckily, Brand X had a *training system* that included a copy of all the same data that was in their live SAP production system. In this training system she could create whatever she wanted, without worrying that she'd be sending sunglasses to customers who hadn't order them.

## 3.1  First try

This time, after she logged on, she clicked on the CREATE SALES ORDERS tile, and the screen to create sales orders appeared (see Figure 3.1).

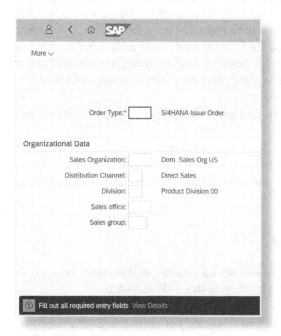

*Figure 3.1: Create sales order screen*

Here's where the fun begins, she thought. She saw a bunch of blank fields and she didn't know what they were for. Vanessa had just rattled off what to put in them yesterday but hadn't said what they did. She saw that ORDER TYPE had an asterisk next to it and she knew that it meant that this was a required field. She opened the training manual and found a section labeled 'Order Types'.

## 3.2    Sales order types

The *sales order type*, or *document type*, is used as a high-level separation of functionality for sales orders. For example, the standard SAP system is delivered with different order types for standard sales, returns, and debit memo requests. Each of these order types controls a different variation of the sales process. When we create a standard order, we expect to sell something, ship out the products, and bill the customer. When we create a return order, we expect to receive products back from the customer and issue a credit. The order type is the highest level of this type of control and, as we'll see later, there are more detailed levels of this type of process control at the *item category* and *schedule line* levels. the sales order type can also be used as a high-level reporting category. There are many other attributes that we can report on, so it's usually best not to create too many document types because we might be dependent on the user to select the right one; the best rule of thumb is to keep it simple. For Brand X, we have copied the standard delivered SAP order types and added a *Z* in front of them so we can adjust them as needed. For example, we created order type 'ZOR' as a copy of the standard order type 'OR'. Happy Ordering!

Ok, that makes sense, thought Lauren. Different order types for things like regular orders versus returns.

What about this ORGANIZATIONAL DATA area? What were all these boxes for?, Lauren asked herself as she opened the training manual and read on.

## 3.3    Enterprise structure

The *enterprise structure* (also known as *organizational data*) is used to model a company's business structure in the SAP software.

For example, a company's legal entities are set up in the SAP system as a *company code*. The organizational data is typically set up in SAP with a short code, which is made up of letters or numbers followed by a longer description. A company code, for example, could be **US01** or **1000** with a description of **Brand X US**. Depending on the type of organizational structure, there may be additional data such as address, currency, or other details that are saved during the setup of the enterprise structure.

The primary purpose of setting up the enterprise structure in SAP is to support reporting. Every time a business transaction occurs, (for example, when a sales order is created), it is recorded in the system as occurring within a certain organizational structure. As a result, reports can easily distinguish between transactions occurring in one organizational structure versus another. For example, revenue earned by the US company versus the Canadian company.

Within the order-to-cash business process, the key organizational structures are: *sales organization, distribution channel,* and *division* (these three together are known as the *sales area*). Other important organizational structures are: *sales district, sales office, sales group, company code,* and *plant*. Let's take a look at each one of these to understand their purpose and use.

## Company code

As mentioned earlier, the company code represents a company's legal entity, and generally corresponds to how a company is legally incorporated. The company code is a finance organizational structure, so while it is not directly used in the SD area, each of our sales organizations falls under a specific company code.

## Sales organization

The sales organization is the selling entity that does business with customers. It is assigned to a company code, and quite often corresponds directly to that company code; i.e., they have a one-to-one relationship. For example, under the US Company code, there might be a US sales organization. At some companies, however, there are multiple sales organizations under a given company code. For example, under the US Company code, there might be USSA (consumer sales) and USGV (government sales). It is important to remember, however, that there are other ways of segmenting sales data, as we'll see below with distribution channel and division. It's best to keep your high-level structures like sales organization as simple as possible.

## Distribution Channel

This is typically thought of as **how** we are selling. Do we have a separate wholesale and retail sales channel? If so, these could be set up as different distribution channels in our enterprise structure. The distribution channel is represented in SAP as a two-digit code, plus a description; for example, *10—Retail*, and *20—Wholesale*.

## Division

The division represents **what** is being sold. It is akin to a very high-level product line. A typical example would be to have one division (let's say '01') for product sales, and another (let's say '02') for services sales. As with all organizational structures, simpler is generally better. There are many ways to group materials (such as 'material groups' and 'product hierarchies') that are not dependent on division.

### Cross-division

 SAP offers the functionality to have a *cross-division*, which is a generic division that can be used to represent any division. This is particularly useful when setting up *master data* (we'll learn more about this later) that is specific to a given division. The use of a cross-division can enable us to set up pricing records specific to the cross-division, which then apply to any division used in our sales orders.

## Sales area

The combination of sales organization, distribution channel, and division is known in SAP-speak as the *sales area*. A great deal of configuration and master data is set up by sales area, which regulates functionality and data for these groupings.

### KISS—Keep It Simple!

 As a general rule, it is best to keep the organizational structures in SAP as simple as possible in order to support business needs. The more complex the organizational structure, the more burden is placed on master data maintenance. Every material and customer master data record created needs to be created in every combination of organizational structures it will be used in. Additionally, the more elaborate the organizational structures, the higher the chance that someone will either pick the wrong one or will be so overwhelmed by choices, that they pick whatever comes first in a list.

### Sales district

This is represents the customers' geography, for sales purposes.

### Sales office

This is used to represent either a physical sales office location or a regional grouping of the sales structure (optional).

### Sales group

This represents a sales grouping under the sales office. For example, if the sales office is 'WE' for West, the sales group could be 'LA' for Los Angeles. Be careful using the sales group to represent individuals. Individual salespeople would be better represented as partners, master-data that is intended to be more dynamic.

None of the following three fields are required, but they can be useful in tracking sales for commission or other purposes:

### Plant

Although not an SD-owned organizational structure, a plant is definitely one we make use of, and should understand. The plant represents where a company's products are made, stored and shipped from. There can be one or many plants and each one is assigned to the sales organization/distribution channel that it is allowed to supply. In configuration settings, we define which plants a sales organization can sell from. For example, the US sales organization might not be allowed to sell from the Canadian plant. Or maybe the distribution channel for wholesale can only be supplied from a central plant, and not a regional one. These types of rules can be built into configuration in a process called *enterprise structure assignment*. Each time we enter a sales-order line item, a plant is indicated on the line to represent where we sell the product from. Additionally, the plant data includes the plant's physical address, which is important in calculating sales taxes because it indicates **where** we are selling the product from.

### Shipping point

This represents where in the warehouse (plant) things are shipped from. For example, there could be one dispatch area for regular items, one for very large items, and another one for returns.

### Storage location

This is also a structure under plant. The storage location represents where, within the plant, materials are physically located. For example, 'finished goods' is a typical storage location from which we check inventory availability when shipping a product.

## 3.4   Sales order creation

So, back to Lauren...

She nodded her head and looked back at her sales order create screen. She clicked on the ORDER TYPE field and on the checkbox that appeared in it. A list of sales order types then popped up (see Figure 3.2).

She noticed that many of them began with Z just like the training manual had said they would. She also noticed that there were numerous other order types. Feeling a little overwhelmed, she wondered if there wasn't a way to limit the choices here and streamline things? Did the company really use 42 different order types? She spotted the ZOR order type that she had used yesterday with Vanessa, and selected it.

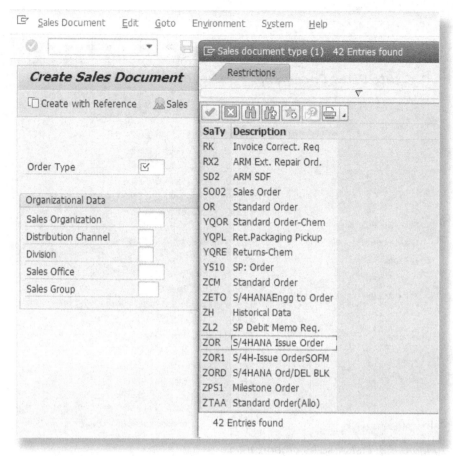

*Figure 3.2: List of order types*

She then clicked on the SALES ORGANIZATION field to bring up a dropdown list of possible sales organizations (see Figure 3.3).

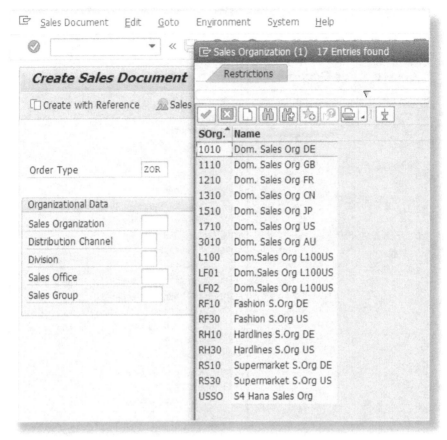

*Figure 3.3: List of sales organizations*

Ok, this was making more sense now. Sales in the US should come from the US sales organization. Vanessa had used 1710 yesterday, and Lauren could see from this list now that 1710 was the US sales organization. She selected 1710 and went through the same process of selecting the DISTRIBUTION CHANNEL and DIVISION. She pressed [Enter] and the sales order screen opened (see Figure 3.4).

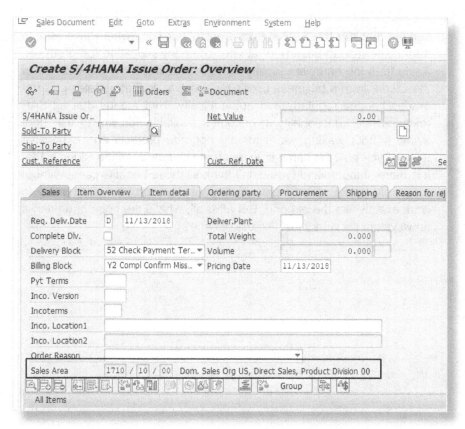

*Figure 3.4: Sales Area in sales order screen*

She noticed that in the sales order there was a row called SALES AREA, and she now knew what that meant! There were the entries she had put in; we are selling from the US Sales organization, via the direct sales distribution channel, for product division 00 (cross-division). Now we're cooking with gas!, as her grandfather used to say.

## The Cloud

You've probably heard of *the Cloud*. These days it seems like everything is moving to the Cloud, delivered from the Cloud, or living in the Cloud; everything is cloud, cloud, cloud! But what does it mean? In the SAP world, your solution is either *cloud-based* or *on-premise*. The computer servers that run the SAP software are either somewhere in a remote data center (cloud-based), or at your company's location (on-premise). Aside from the hardware location and cost savings, the big promise of the Cloud, from a business user's perspective, is that updates and upgrades happen regularly and automatically. That means that as SAP releases new functionality, it becomes available for you to use right away, without waiting years for big upgrade projects and expensive testing cycles. At the same time, another key feature of the Cloud is that it is more standardized (you didn't think all those benefits came without a cost did you?), which means the new system probably isn't going to work exactly like the old one. But after all, what's the point of getting a new system if it works just like the old one?

# 4 Master data

In this chapter, we introduce the concept of *master data* and how it is used in the Sales and Distribution module. We'll discuss what master data is and dive into some of the most important master data objects, business partners and material masters. We'll then see how they interact with sales orders, and finish up with pricing.

Lauren was ready to continue creating her sales order. She had entered the order type and the sales area information. She knew the first thing she needed to do was to enter the customer. She remembered from yesterday that the customer went in the SOLD-TO PARTY field, so she clicked on the magnifying glass icon to bring up the search help screen (see Figure 4.1).

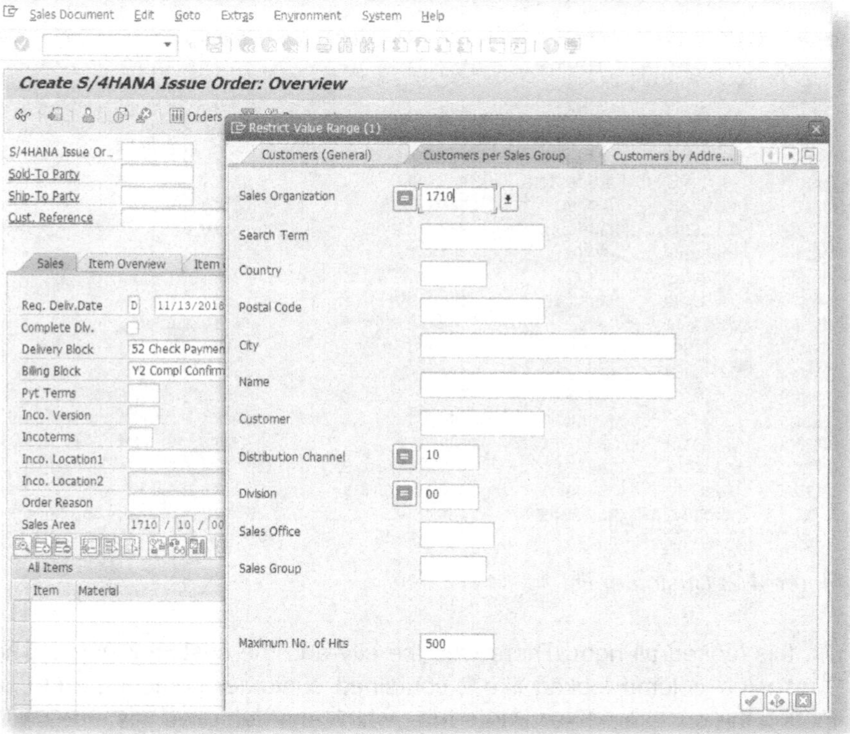

*Figure 4.1: Sold-To Party search*

She noticed that when the screen opened, the data in it defaulted to the sales area data she had entered in the previous screen. She correctly assumed that this would help her search US customers only (SALES ORGANIZATION: 1710). She clicked on the green check mark icon   and a list of customers popped up (see Figure 4.2).

| SearchTerm | Cty | PostalCode | City | Name 1 | Customer | DChl | Dv | SOff. | SGrp |
|---|---|---|---|---|---|---|---|---|---|
| BASE-10001 | US | 30002 | AVONDALE ESTATES | OFFICE SUPPLY | USCU02 | 10 | 00 | | |
| BASE-10002 | US | 30003 | NORCROSS | R2R SUPPLY | USCU03 | 10 | 00 | | |
| BIKES | US | 94302 | PALO ALTO | SPORTS BIKES INC. | USCU_L11 | 10 | 00 | | |
| CBK01 | US | 10007 | NEW YORK | SKYMART CORP | USCU_L01 | 10 | 00 | | |
| CBK01 | US | 10035 | NEW YORK | FAST BIKES INC.. | USCUST01-L | 10 | 00 | | |
| CBK02 | US | 19801 | WILMINGTON | TOYS4U | USCU_L02 | 10 | 00 | | |
| CBK03 | US | 21202 | BALTIMORE | VIADOX | USCU_L03 | 10 | 00 | | |
| CBK04 | US | 15219 | PITTSBURGH | PERFORMANCE BIKES | USCU_S01 | 10 | 00 | | |
| CBK05 | US | 02109 | BOSTON | CUSTOM SPORTS | USCU_S02 | 10 | 00 | | |
| CBK06 | US | 15601 | GREENSBURG | EASTSIDE BIKES | USCU_S03 | 10 | 00 | | |
| CBK07 | US | 04101 | PORTLAND | FIT CYCLES | USCU_S04 | 10 | 00 | | |
| CBK08 | US | 06103 | HARTFORD | GREATER HARTFORD AREA | USCU_S05 | 10 | 00 | | |
| CBK09 | US | 10017 | MANHATTAN | HUB & SPOKES INC | USCU_S06 | 10 | 00 | | |
| CBK10 | US | 27603 | RALEIGH | QUOTEX | USCU_L04 | 10 | 00 | | |
| CBK11 | US | 29401 | CHARLESTON | BLUESTAR CORP | USCU_L05 | 10 | 00 | | |
| CBK12 | US | 37201 | NASHVILLE | DEXON | USCU_L06 | 10 | 00 | | |
| CBK13 | US | 33128 | MIAMI | INTERLUDE INC | USCU_L07 | 10 | 00 | | |
| CBK14 | US | 30303 | ATLANTA | VERACITY | USCU_L08 | 10 | 00 | | |
| CBK15 | US | 27603 | RALEIGH | WESTEND CYCLES | USCU_S07 | 10 | 00 | | |
| CBK17 | US | 37201 | NASHVILLE | GREENHIGH BIKES | USCU_S09 | 10 | 00 | | |
| CBK18 | US | 33128 | MIAMI | TURBO BIKES | USCU_S10 | 10 | 00 | | |
| CBK19 | US | 30303 | ATLANTA | BIKE WORLD | USCU_S11 | 10 | 00 | | |
| CBK20 | US | 23218 | RICHMOND | CENTURY CYCLES | USCU_S12 | 10 | 00 | | |
| CBK21 | US | 36104 | MONTGOMERY | ROLLING BIKE SHOP | USCU_S13 | 10 | 00 | | |
| CBK22 | US | 48226 | DETROIT | BIGMART | USCU_L09 | 10 | 00 | | |
| CBK23 | US | 44114 | PUBLIC SQUARE | COSTCLUB | USCU_L10 | 10 | 00 | | |
| CBK24 | US | 60602 | CHICAGO | CITYSCAPE CYCLES | USCU_S14 | 10 | 00 | | |
| CBK25 | US | 50306 | DES MOINES | NORTHSIDE BIKES | USCU_S15 | 10 | 00 | | |
| CBK26 | US | 53202 | MILWAUKEE | GOGO BIKES | USCU_S16 | 10 | 00 | | |

*Figure 4.2: Customer list*

Ok, this looked all right. There was the city and the customer name. The CUSTOMER column looked like it contained customer numbers; and she spotted the customer FAST BIKES INC., which she had used yesterday with Vanessa. She selected Fast Bikes, pressed  Enter  a couple of times, and all of sudden her sales order screen had a lot of new data on it (see Figure 4.3).

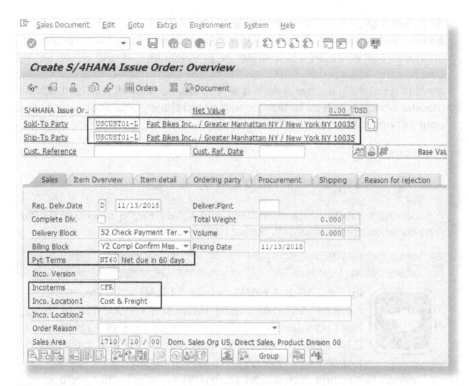

*Figure 4.3: Sales order screen with customer details*

Now, she saw that there were address details, an entry in the SHIP-TO PAR-TY field, and entries in the PYT TERMS and INCOTERMS fields. All that must be coming from the customer master. But where was that and how did it get there? She reached for the manual and read on.

## 4.1 Master data concept

Imagine your favorite e-commerce site. Now imagine that every time you order something on it you have to re-enter your name, your email, your shipping address, your billing address, and your payment information. Kind of a pain, right? Most likely, you don't have to do this. You just log in and all your information shows up. That's because the first time you sign up to buy something all of your information gets saved, so that when you come back, it just takes a few clicks and that new Chia pet is on its way to your home. That's because your name, address, and all those details are saved as *master data*. Now imagine that every time a company sold you something they had to manually enter the price, the weight, the dimensions, and the description of that product into the sale order. That wouldn't make a lot of sense. So instead, all of that product information is saved as master data so that all that is required is to enter the product number, and all the details flow into the sales order. SAP calls the product information *material master data*. In a nutshell, master data is a way to save a heck of a lot of repetitive manual work, as well as to help ensure **consistency** and **accuracy** of that data throughout the sales process.

## 4.2   Business partners—who's who?

A customer's master data is entered and saved into a *business partner* (known as *customer master* in earlier SAP releases).

### The business partner—new in SAP S/4HANA

 In the SAP S/4 HANA version of SAP software, management of customer master data (and vendor master data) has undergone a significant change. In earlier releases of SAP software, customer data was stored and managed in a customer master. The customer master has a specific set of views, fields, and transaction codes (VD01/XD01) that were used to manage it. Similarly, on the purchasing side, *vendor master* records are created with a different set of transaction codes and views. In SAP S/4HANA, SAP has taken a slightly different approach, treating both customers and vendors as *business partners*. A business partner is an entity that a company does business with—they have a name, an address, and other details. The business partner also has a role assigned to them. They may have a customer role, a vendor role, a bank role, or any number of roles. More importantly, any given business partner can have multiple roles assigned to it. Each role needs different fields maintained for it. As a result, the creation of business partners now has just one shared transaction code (BP) and one set of screens to work with. Within that transaction, the business partner can be created and maintained with various roles.

Business partners, such as customers, can be created, displayed, or changed within the Business Partner transaction. Let's go through the creation of a new business partner so that we can highlight a few key concepts.

When we first create a customer, it is with the *organization* category (as opposed to person category). The most important concept to understand at this point is contained in the CREATE IN BP ROLE field. This tells us what role we are creating for this business partner. Are we creating them as a customer? as a vendor? as a bank? As you can see in the drop-down list, there is a multitude of roles in which a partner can be created (see Figure 4.4).

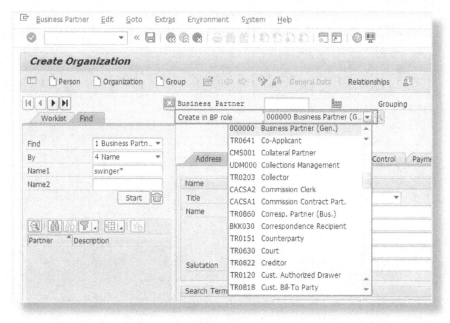

*Figure 4.4: Create business partner*

It's important to understand that the roles are not necessarily exclusive. We can create a business partner as both a customer and a vendor, for instance. In such a situation, some of the data is common to both of the roles. For example, regardless of whether the partner is in a customer or vendor role, it still has the same name and corporate address. However, there is data that is role-specific; the customer role could have certain price groups assigned, or a default delivering plant. The vendor role could have specific purchasing groups assigned.

In our example, we first create the business partner with a general role, and we enter general details such as name and address (see Figure 4.5). We then enter a customer role, where we maintain sales-specific information. You may also have noticed the GROUPING field. We use this to define the *number range,* which is the way SAP numbers the particular object. In this case, if we leave the GROUPING field blank, SAP will use an *internal* number range, which is a pre-defined, default number range, for business partners. If we want to use a specific number range, we can make the desired selection in the GROUPING field.

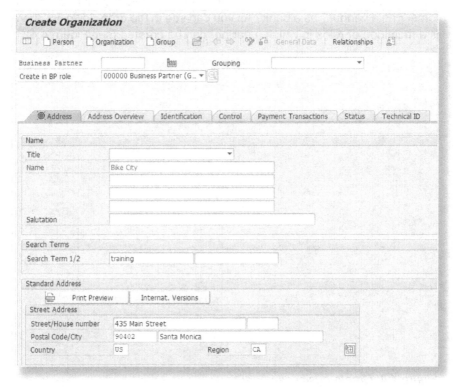

*Figure 4.5: Create business partner name and address*

Here, we are creating a new customer called *Bike City*. We've selected the BP role of BUSINESS PARTNER (GENERAL), and entered the NAME, STREET ADDRESS details, and SEARCH TERMS (used for easy searching). You may notice that the ADDRESS tab has a red circle n it, indicating that something is not complete. SAP has the quirky habit of only validating what you've input after you press the [Enter] key. Once we press [Enter], the system tells us if anything is wrong or missing. Note that next to the ADDRESS tab there are a number of other tabs for data such as ADDRESS OVERVIEW, IDENTIFICATION, CONTROL, etc. Don't despair! Most of the information is optional and is not mandatory. If any field is required, the system highlights this when you try to save the record.

When we save the record, note that our business partner now has a number, and we are automatically put into display mode (see Figure 4.6).

*Figure 4.6: Business partner created*

We have now created a general business partner, but if we want to sell to them as a customer, or buy from them as a vendor, we need to do more. So, we go into change mode, and then select the customer business role in the CHANGE IN BP ROLE field (see Figure 4.7).

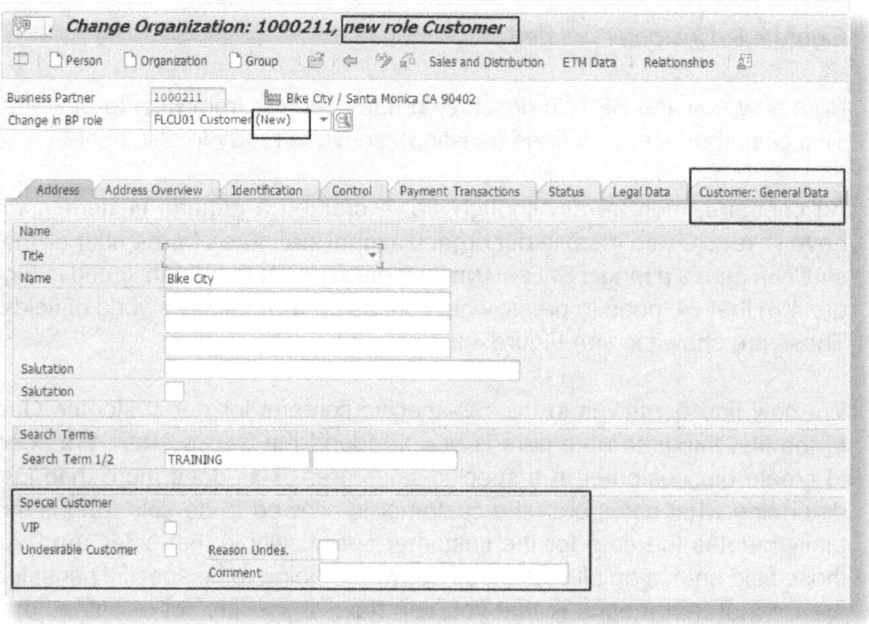

*Figure 4.7: Create customer business role*

You'll notice that as we do this, a new set of tabs appears, as well as some new fields related to customers. The system also indicates that we are cre-ating a NEW role for this business partner in the current transaction. These indicators change after we create them in the role. Once we've saved this new role, we will have a new customer (see Figure 4.8).

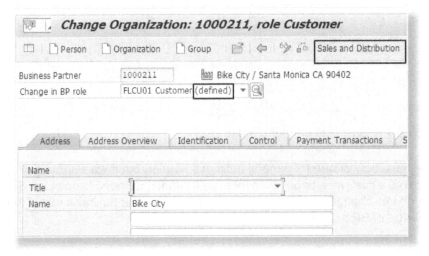

*Figure 4.8: Customer created*

Note now how the BP role description has changed from NEW to DEFINED. This customer is now defined (existing), so we're ready to sell, right?

Au contraire, mon frère! Although we've created a general customer, we haven't yet created them in our organizational structures (remember all that stuff?). There's a magic SALES AND DISTRIBUTION button (highlighted in Figure 4.8) that we need to press, which opens up a whole new world of fields. These are shown in see Figure 4.9.

We now find ourselves in the SD-specific screens for our customer. One of the first things to note here is our old friend the SALES AREA. We need to create our customer in a specific sales area. This does more than just determine what sales area the customer is allowed to be sold from; it actually creates the data for the customer specifically in that sales area. All those field entries on all those tabs above are going to be specific per sales area. What that means is that you can have a specific set of entries that is different per sales area for the same customer. So, rather than having to recreate the same customer for wholesale and retail, or for the US and Canada, for example, you can have the same customer number but with different settings per sales area. But why would you care about that? Well, besides improved data maintenance and accuracy, this gives you the ability to easily do aggregated reporting. For example, to see how much we've sold to Bike City in the US, or in Canada, or in North America, or globally. All this is easy if you use the same customer number. Of course, you don't have to do it this way, and many companies create a different customer record for each country.

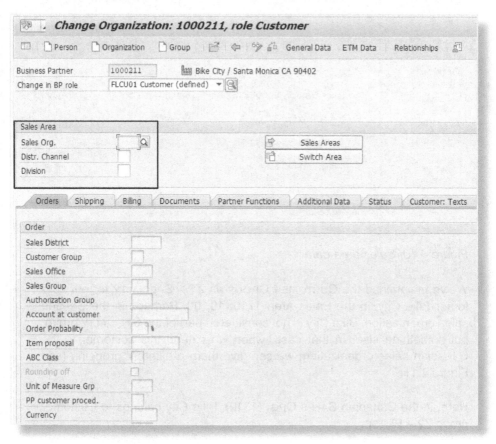

*Figure 4.9: Customer SD fields*

Let's now create our customer for a particular sales area by entering the sales area data. Once we do that, the fields below are no longer grayed out and we can make entries (see Figure 4.10).

51

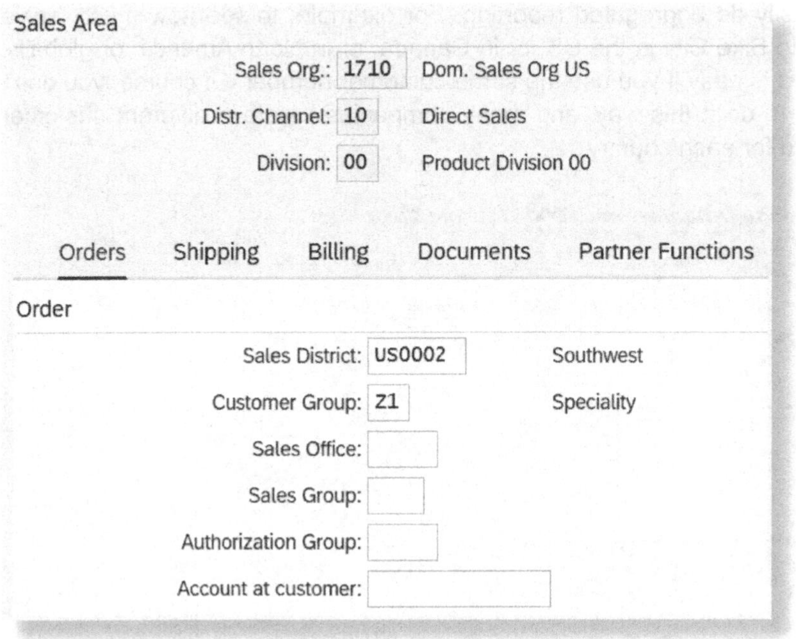

| Sales Area | | |
|---|---|---|
| Sales Org.: | 1710 | Dom. Sales Org US |
| Distr. Channel: | 10 | Direct Sales |
| Division: | 00 | Product Division 00 |

Orders    Shipping    Billing    Documents    Partner Functions

Order

| | | |
|---|---|---|
| Sales District: | US0002 | Southwest |
| Customer Group: | Z1 | Speciality |
| Sales Office: | | |
| Sales Group: | | |
| Authorization Group: | | |
| Account at customer: | | |

*Figure 4.10: Sales area data*

We've maintained the CUSTOMER GROUP as Z1 – SPECIALTY for our cus-tomer Bike City, in the Sales Area 1710, 10, 00. Perhaps in the Canada sales organization, Bike City is not considered part of the SPECIALTY group, but something else. In that case, when we extend this customer to the Canadian sales organization, we can give them a different grouping (see Figure 4.11).

Here, in the Canadian SALES ORG. (1310), Bike City belongs to Customer group Z2 – LARGE.

We won't go into every field on the customer business partner screens now, but as you can see, there are a lot of them! However, with the limited infor-mation that we've filled out, we should now have a customer master that we can work with on a sales order.

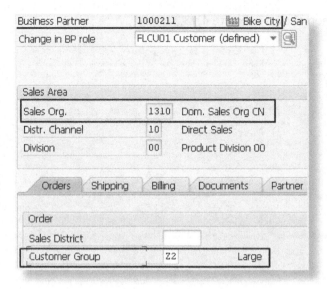

Figure 4.11: Customer in Canadian sales area

## 4.2.1 Business partner in action

Lauren looked up from the manual and rubbed her temples. The concept made sense, but those screens looked so busy, with countless fields and tabs. She remembered what Vanessa had said yesterday about GUI versus Fiori. Maybe the Fiori screen looked better. She decided to take a look. She found the MAINTAIN BUSINESS PARTNER tile on her launchpad and double clicked on it (see Figure 4.12).

Figure 4.12: Fiori—Maintain Business Partner tile

This opened the screen shown in Figure 4.13.

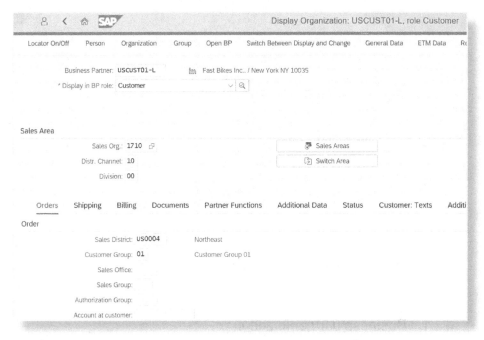

*Figure 4.13: Fiori screen—display business partner, role Customer*

Using what she learned from the manual, she decided to view a partner with a customer role in the US sales area. It looked a little less intimidating, and a bit more like a web page, but still pretty darn busy. She hoped she wouldn't have to know all this information right away. She decided she would try to find those fields that had defaulted into the sales order…what were they again? Oh yes, PAYMENT TERMS and INCOTERMS. Payment terms sounded like it was related to billing, so she clicked on BILLING in order to look at the billing-related fields (see Figure 4.14).

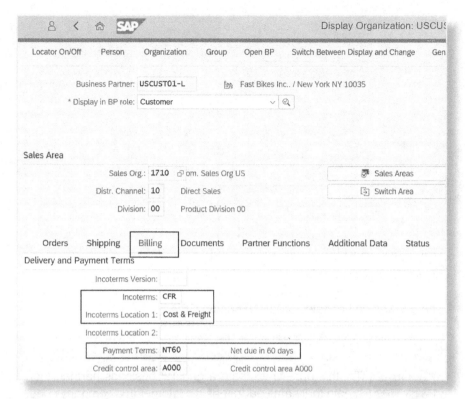

*Figure 4.14: Business partner customer billing details*

She saw that the PAYMENT TERMS were set as NT 60, and the INCOTERMS were set at CFR. That made sense; it was what she saw on the sales order when she was testing. Whatever values are put on the customer master are pulled into the same fields on the sales order (see Figure 4.15).

*Figure 4.15 : Sales order*

There it was on her sales order, NT60 and CFR.

**Create your own customer business partner**

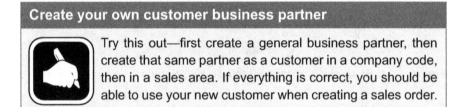

Try this out—first create a general business partner, then create that same partner as a customer in a company code, then in a sales area. If everything is correct, you should be able to use your new customer when creating a sales order.

Following the directions in the manual, Lauren created a new customer. As an added twist, she gave it a colorful payment term of *0007* (almost James Bond) and left the INCOTERMS blank to see what would happen. Ok, let's see if this works, she thought to herself.

Starting the sales order creation process again, she input her new customer into her sales order (see Figure 4.16).

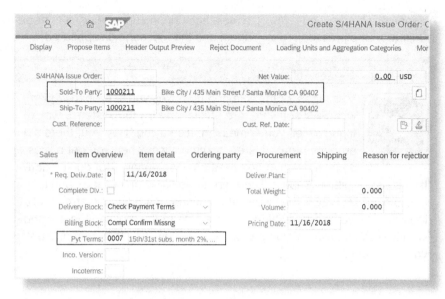

Figure 4.16: Lauren's test order

It worked! There was her new customer, Bike City, and the payment terms (PYT. TERMS) appeared as 0007. The INCOTERMS field was blank. She wondered if she could manually input the INCOTERMS, so she gave it a try (see Figure 4.17).

| S/4HANA Issue Order: | | Net Value: | 0.00 USD |
| Sold-To Party: 1000211 | Bike City / 435 Main Street / Santa Monica CA 90402 | | |
| Ship-To Party: 1000211 | Bike City / 435 Main Street / Santa Monica CA 90402 | | |
| Cust. Reference: | | Cust. Ref. Date: | |

Sales   Item Overview   Item detail   Ordering party   Procurement   Shipping   Reason for rejection

* Req. Deliv.Date: D   11/16/2018
Complete Dlv.: ☐
Delivery Block: Check Payment Terms
Billing Block: Compl Confirm Missng
Pyt Terms: 0007  15th/31st subs. month 2%, ...
Inco. Version:
Incoterms: CPT
Inco. Location1: Los Angeles

Information

ⓘ  Freight is redetermined

Figure 4.17: Incoterms –manually input

As soon as she pressed [Enter], a message popped up—FREIGHT IS REDE-TERMINED. She pressed [Enter] again and the message disappeared.

---

## Messages

 Messages, or the little pop-up boxes you see when working with SAP software, are ubiquitous. It's the system's way of trying to tell you something. It's saying "Hey you, there's a problem here!". Here's some advice: when you get a mes-sage, stay calm and read on. Don't panic. But don't ignore the message either. Read it. There are three types of message and they indicate the severity of the issue: informational, warning, and error. If you look closely, you'll see a little I, W, or E next to the message text. I and W messages go away if you press [Enter]. However, to get rid of the E, you have to fix something!

---

It was lunchtime, so Lauren she decided she would continue later. She wondered if she could save this order. She clicked on the save button in the lower right corner (not shown here) to see what would happen, and up popped a box indicating DOCUMENT INCOMPLETE (see Figure 4.18).

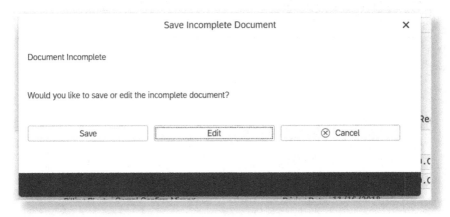

*Figure 4.18: Save Incomplete Document pop-up window*

She clicked on EDIT to see what it would do and was taken to the screen shown in Figure 4.19.

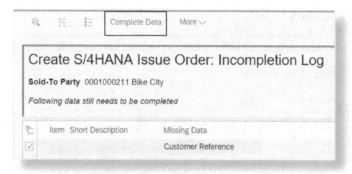

Figure 4.19: Complete Data screen

Hmm, INCOMPLETION LOG. MISSING DATA for CUSTOMER REFERENCE. Ah, that's right, she had forgotten to put in the customer's PO number. She clicked on the COMPLETE DATA button and it took her to the CUSTOMER REFERENCE field. She typed in *TBD*, then went back and tried to save the order again. This time it saved, and the system showed the order number at the bottom left of the screen (see Figure 4.20).

Figure 4.20: Order saved

Phew! Now time for lunch.

## The incompletion procedure

 A standard part of all SD processes is the *incompletion procedure*. This procedure is a set of rules to ensure that you have supplied all the necessary data before you can move on to the next step. After all, you wouldn't want to get to the shipping stage, only to find out that you were missing the customer's address, right? The incompletion procedure is configurable, and allows you to control which fields are checked , and the severity of the message.

## 4.3 Partner functions in SD

Feeling well-fed and recharged, Lauren sat down again to review her order (see Figure 4.21).

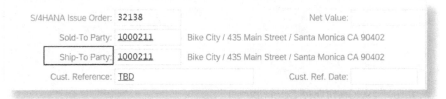

| S/4HANA Issue Order: | 32138 | Net Value: |
| Sold-To Party: | 1000211 | Bike City / 435 Main Street / Santa Monica CA 90402 |
| Ship-To Party: | 1000211 | Bike City / 435 Main Street / Santa Monica CA 90402 |
| Cust. Reference: | TBD | Cust. Ref. Date: |

*Figure 4.21: Test order*

She saw her order number and her fake PO number, TBD. But there was one remaining question about the data that had defaulted in from the customer master. Where did this SHIP-TO PARTY come from? And why was it the same number and name as the SOLD-TO PARTY? She reached for the manual again...

**Partner Functions**

The SD module uses the concept of *partner functions*. In SD processes, partner data is always identified with the role it plays in the OTC business process. There are four key partner roles (and lots of minor ones) in SD: *sold-to, ship-to, bill-to,* and *payer.* Standard sales processes require that all of these partners are present and identified on the sales order. Let's take a look at what they are used for:

▶ **Sold-to party**—the partner that is buying from us; the key partner in the OTC process.

▶ **Ship-to party**—the partner to whom we are shipping.

▶ **Bill-to party**—the partner to whom we are sending the invoice.

▶ **Payer**—the partner who is paying the bill. They are the one against whom the accounts receivable is recorded, and whose credit is checked.

You can see an overview in Figure 4.22.

| Partn.Funct. | | Partner | Name | Street | Postal C... | Cty |
|---|---|---|---|---|---|---|
| ☐ | Sold-To Party | ⌄ 1000211 | Bike City | 435 Main Street | 90402 | Santa Monica |
| ☐ | Bill-To Party | ⌄ 1000211 | Bike City | 435 Main Street | 90402 | Santa Monica |
| ☐ | Payer | ⌄ 1000211 | Bike City | 435 Main Street | 90402 | Santa Monica |
| ☐ | Ship-To Party | ⌄ 1000211 | Bike City | 435 Main Street | 90402 | Santa Monica |

*Figure 4.22: Partner functions*

When we first create a customer, all four partner functions are also automatically created; all with the same number and address details. As you can see in the screenshot, when we created Bike City, it was created with customer number 1000211 and an address, which were copied to all four partner functions. For many customers this is sufficient—there is only one name and address for selling, shipping, billing, and paying. However, for some customers, we need to maintain different partner data. Consider a retail customer with many different store locations. The ship-to location would probably be an individual store address, but the payer might be the corporate office. The sold-to and bill-to addresses could be the store, a corporate location, or another address, depending on how we want to work with the customer. We have the option of creating multiple shipping, billing, and payer details, as required. Once they are created, they can then be assigned to our sold-to customer on the PARTNER FUNCTIONS tab of the customer business partner, for their respective sales area (see Figure 4.23).

| | Orders | Shipping | Billing | Documents | Partner Functions | Additional Data | Status | Customer: |
|---|---|---|---|---|---|---|---|---|

Partner Functions

| | PR | Partner Functn | Number | Descript. | Partner description | Def |
|---|---|---|---|---|---|---|
| ○ | SP | Sold-To Party | 1000211 | Bike City | | ☐ |
| ○ | BP | Bill-To Party | 1000211 | Bike City | | ☐ |
| ○ | PY | Payer | 1000211 | Bike City | | ☐ |
| ○ | SH | Ship-To Party | 1000211 | Bike City | | ☑ |
| ○ | SH | Ship-To Party | USCU_S11 | Bike World | Alternate shipping location | ☐ |
| ○ | | | | | | ☐ |

*Figure 4.23: Partner Functions tab*

In the example shown, we have added a second ship-to party to our Bike City customer master. We've also selected a checkbox to indicate that the Bike City location is the DEF (default) ship-to location.

When we create a sales order for Bike City, we now have the option of selecting either of the two ship-to locations. In the sales order, we get a pop-up window asking us to choose which ship-to party we want to use on the order, and the default location is pre-selected (see Figure 4.24).

*Figure 4.24: Ship-to party pop-up window*

If we select the alternative ship-to party, Bike World, we can see that the address is now shown in our sales order partner's details (see Figure 4.25).

*Figure 4.25: Alternative Ship-To Party*

Once we've selected the alternative SHIP-TO PARTY, it then appears on our sales order screen. By clicking on the magnifying glass icon (highlighted in the image), we are taken to the PARTNER tab on the HEADER DATA screen, where we can see all the partners on our sales order, and further details (see Figure 4.26).

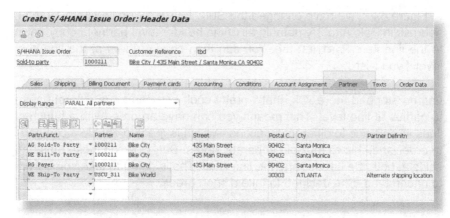

Figure 4.26: Header Data—Partner tab

Here we can see our four mandatory partners, and that the SHIP-TO PARTY for this order is Bike World in Atlanta, and not the Bike City address in Santa Monica. Similarly, we can change the BILL-TO PARTY and PAYER on this screen, if desired. We can also add additional partners such as a freight forwarding agent, a sales rep, or any party involved in the transaction who you would like to track or include in the sales process.

SAP also enables you to set partners at item level. For example, individual sales order line items might ship to different locations. In this case, you are able to set a different ship-to party at the line item level

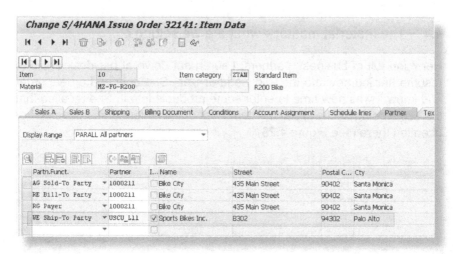

Figure 4.27: Item level partners

In Figure 4.27, we have changed the SHIP-TO PARTY on line item 10 to an address in Palo Alto. By default, all of the header level partners copy down to the line item PARTNER tab. You can then change them at the line item level if you wish.

Lauren stopped there. Ok, that's pretty cool; you can have different ship-to parties at line level. This means you can have an order with a bunch of lines all shipping to different locations—which is great to enable a company to order and ship to multiple separate stores. But, wow, all those tabs and fields at both the header and the line level! That's going to take some work to understand. She decided to take a short break.

## One-time customers

 Sometimes we don't have the time or need to create a full customer master. Think of a retail scenario, for example. We wouldn't want to tell the customer to wait while we fill out a whole lot of unnecessary information. To support this, SAP has long had the concept of the *one-time customer*. This is a special type of business partner that is created in advance, and every time it is entered on a sales order, it triggers a pop-up screen asking only for the most basic information. The same one-time customer number can be used over and over again.

## 4.4 The material master—what are we selling?

Her mind full of business partners, Lauren sat down at her desk again to resume her journey into the wild world of SAP. She opened her test order and knew it was now time to enter some products into it. She recalled that the items being sold were at the item level of the order so she directed her attention there (see Figure 4.28).

| Item | Material | Item Description | Order Quantity | First Date | Delivery Priority | Plnt | Storage location | Ship./Re... | Route |
|------|----------|------------------|----------------|------------|-------------------|------|------------------|-------------|-------|
| | | | | 12/12/2018 | | | | | |
| | | | | 12/12/2018 | | | | | |
| | | | | 12/12/2018 | | | | | |

Sales Area: 1710 / 10 / 00 Dom. Sales Org US, Direct Sales, Product Division 00

All Items

*Figure 4.28: Item entry*

She saw that she could do a drop-down help search on the MATERIAL column, so she searched and selected a bike material to see what would happen (see Figure 4.29).

*Figure 4.29: First item*

After entering the material, the item row was automatically completed with a large amount of data. She correctly surmised that, just like the business partner master data, this information was stored on a master record that got pulled in to her order. She double clicked on the material number and was taken to the sales order ITEM DATA screen (see Figure 4.30).

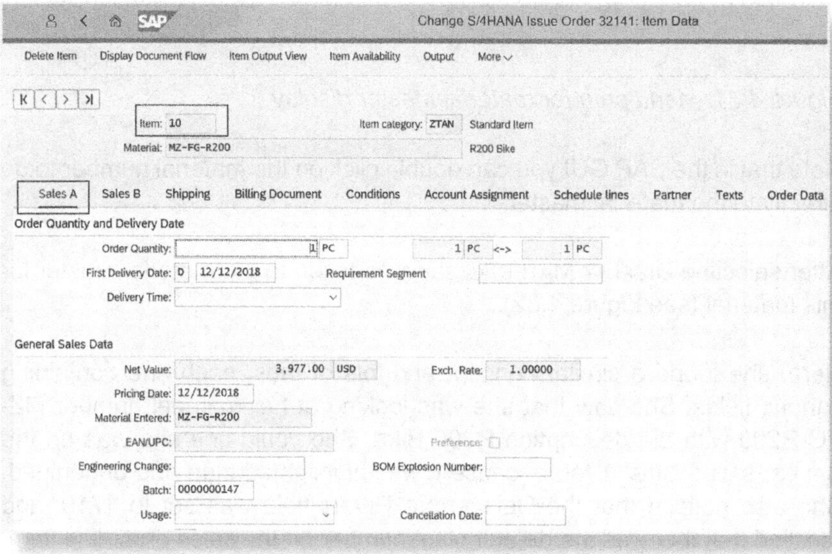

*Figure 4.30: Sales order item data*

She could see that she was looking at ITEM 10 (by default, sales order items are numbered in increments of 10) and that she was on the SALES A tab. She could see that there were many fields here, and there were also many other tabs, including the PARTNER tab that she had reviewed earlier. She wanted to take a look at the material master itself and wondered if she had to go through a separate transaction, or if she could get to it directly from

here. After clicking around a bit she found it under the menu path MORE •
DISPLAY MATERIAL (see Figure 4.31).

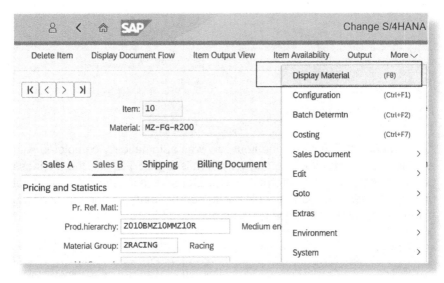

*Figure 4.31: Menu path for material master display*

Note that in the SAP GUI you can double click on the material number to go
directly to the material master.

After selecting DISPLAY MATERIAL she was taken to the material master for
this material (see Figure 4.32).

Here, she found a similar concept and lots of tabs, each one containing
various fields. She saw that she was looking at her material number MZ-
FG-R200 with the description R200 BIKE. She could see she was on the
SALES: SALES ORG. 1 tab because it was highlighted blue and underlined.
She also noticed that the DELIVERING PLANT field was set to 1710, and
recalled that that was the default plant number on the sales order line item.
She browsed through the different tabs of the material master and saw all
kinds of data. Some data made sense to her, such as weights and plants,
and there was some that she had no idea about, such as MRP groups and
valuation types. But overall, it made sense—save all the details on a master
record, and then it all gets pulled into the sales order 'auto-magically'.

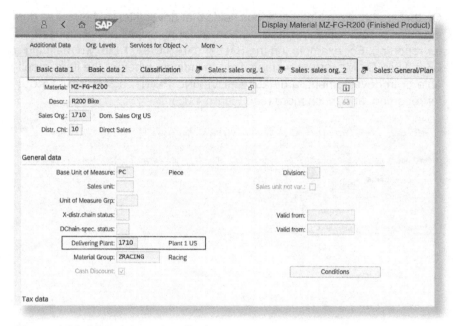

*Figure 4.32: Material master display*

She then turned to her training guide to learn more about the material master.

## 4.4.1 Materials

The material master is the most cross-functional piece of master data in the system. Every team and process stream has an interest or activity related to materials. When materials are created, they are created as a certain *material type;* for example, finished goods, raw material, trading goods, etc. The material type controls some basic functionality, such as which tabs and fields are available on the screens.

There are three tabs on the material master that belong to SD:

▶ SALES: SALES ORG. 1

▶ SALES: SALES ORG. 2

▶ SALES: GENERAL/PLANT

On these tabs, we maintain various fields that drive different behaviors during sales order, delivery, and billing transactions, as well as categorizations for reporting. For example, on the SALES: SALES ORG. 1 tab, we maintain a BASE UNIT OF MEASURE, a status field to indicate whether the item is sellable or in development, a default DELIVERING PLANT, a MATERIAL GROUP for reporting, and much more (see Figure 4.33).

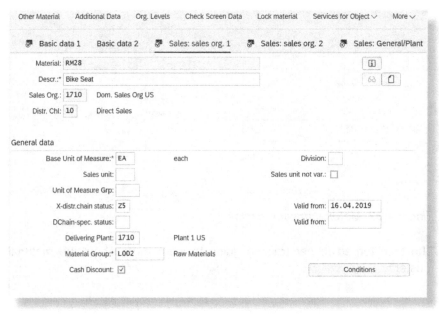

*Figure 4.33: Material master—Sales: sales org 1 tab*

Likewise, on the SALES: SALES ORG. 2 tab, there are numerous field options (see Figure 4.34). The MATERIAL PRICE GRP field can be used to create groupings of like materials, for pricing purposes. The ACCT ASSMT GRP MAT (account assignment group) field is used to drive revenue account determination during billing. Other fields, such as the ITEM CATEGORY GROUP, are key in driving the item category that appears on the sales order; if the material is a finished good, it might have one item category group, as opposed to another material that represents a service.

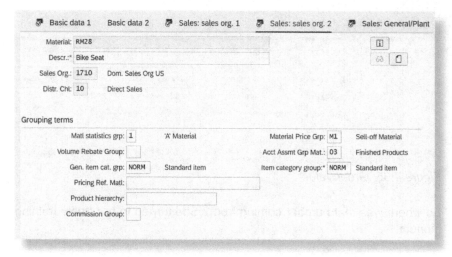

*Figure 4.34: Material master—Sales: sales org 2 tab*

As with business partners, the material master data is created specifically within organizational structures. This means, for example, that the same material number can have different field entries in one sales organization versus another.

Lauren nodded her head. Master data was beginning to make sense. But there was one thing she was looking for on the material master that she couldn't find—the price.

## 4.5  Pricing—how much is it?

Lauren went back to her sales order. She could see that after entering her line item, the order now had a price of $3,977, but she couldn't see where it was coming from—she hadn't found that price on the material master anywhere (see Figure 4.35).

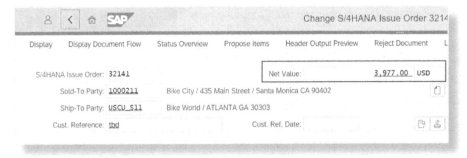

*Figure 4.35: Order value*

So where was that number coming from? She turned to her trusty training manual.

### Sales pricing

As with business partners and materials, pricing is driven by master data. However, it differs in that the pricing on a sales order is determined via the *condition technique*.

---

**The condition technique**

 The condition technique is an SAP method of finding the right data at the right time. It is essentially a set of configured business rules. It is used throughout the SD module for things such pricing, output determination, account determination, free goods, and lots more. The condition technique is flexible, structured, and robust, which is why it is relied on to such a large extent. So what is it? Sometimes called the *search strategy*, it's the way SAP can be structured through configuration (no coding required!) to pull in the right data, at the right time. It is a procedure which is made up of a list of *condition types*. Each condition type contains an *access sequence* which has a list of tables that are searched through to find the right data (*condition record*). Condition records themselves are master data typically created by end users.

---

In the sales order, the first step is to determine a pricing procedure. The pricing procedure is made up of a sequence of pricing condition types. Each pricing condition type is made up of a sequence of *pricing tables*, and each pricing table has a set of prices (pricing condition records). The end goal is to pull the right data (price) into the order (see Figure 4.36).

**Change View "Procedures - Control Data": Overview**

New Entries

Dialog Structure
- Procedures
  - Procedures - Control

Procedure    Y17101 Materials (US)

Procedures - Control Data

Reference Step Overview

| Step | Co... | Co... | Description | F... | T... | Ma... | R... | St... | Print Code | Sub... | Requir... | Alt.Cal... | Alt.Co... | Acc... |
|---|---|---|---|---|---|---|---|---|---|---|---|---|---|---|
| 10 | 0 | PC01 | Actual Costs | | | ✓ | | | | B | 2 | | | ERL |
| 20 | 0 | PPR0 | Price | | | | ✓ | | | | 2 | | | ERL |
| 25 | 0 | YB01 | Special Surcharge | | | | | | X | 4 | 2 | | | ERL |
| 60 | 0 | PMP0 | Manual Price | | | ✓ | | | | | 2 | | | ERL |
| 70 | 0 | ZMB0 | Goodwill / Guarantee | | | | | | | | | | | ERS |
| 100 | 0 | | Gross Value | | | | | | a | 1 | | 2 | | |
| 120 | 0 | DPG1 | Cust. Grp / Material | | | | | | a | | 2 | | | YB2 |
| 130 | 0 | DCM1 | Customer/Material | | | | | | a | | 2 | | | YB2 |
| 140 | 0 | DC01 | Division / Customer | | | | | | a | | 2 | | | YB2 |
| 145 | 0 | YK07 | Customer Discount | | | | | | b | | 2 | | | YB2 |
| 150 | 0 | ZM01 | Material | | | | | | a | | 2 | | | YB1 |
| 160 | 0 | DPG2 | Customer Price Group | | | | | | a | | 2 | | | YB2 |
| 170 | 0 | DPG3 | Material Price Group | | | | | | a | | 2 | | | YB1 |
| 180 | 0 | DPG4 | Customer/Mat.Pr.Grp | | | | | | a | | 2 | | | YB2 |
| 190 | 0 | DPG5 | Cust. Grp/Mat.Pr.Grp | | | | | | a | | 2 | | | YB2 |
| 200 | 0 | DRG1 | % Gross Amount 1 | 100 | | ✓ | | | a | | 2 | | | YB3 |
| 210 | 0 | DRN1 | % Net Amount 1 | | | ✓ | | | a | | 2 | | | YB3 |
| 220 | 0 | DRQ1 | +/- as to Quantity 1 | | | ✓ | | | a | | 2 | | | YB3 |
| 230 | 0 | DRV1 | Fixed Amount 1 | | | ✓ | | | a | | 2 | | | YB3 |
| 240 | 0 | DRW1 | +/- as to Grss Wght1 | | | ✓ | | | a | | 2 | | | YB3 |
| 300 | 0 | | Sum Surcharges/Discoun.. | 101 | 299 | | | | | | | | | |
| 310 | 0 | PMP0 | | | | ✓ | | | | | 2 | 6 | 3 | ERL |

*Figure 4.36: Pricing procedure*

In this example, we see a pricing procedure called Y17101 – MATERIALS (US). From the description, we can guess that this pricing procedure is probably for the sale of materials in the US. We might also infer that different countries may be set up to use a different procedure, and perhaps services might have a different procedure as well.

Under the procedure there is a long list of four-character codes with a sequential list of STEP numbers. These codes are the pricing condition types. It's not visible here, but under each of the condition types is a list of pricing tables you can search through. This list is called the *access sequence*.

Let's look at an example: a sales order is created and the customer is entered. Behind the scenes, the pricing procedure is immediately determined, based on a field on the sales order document type (*document pricing procedure field*), a field on the customer master (*pricing procedure field*), and the sales area of the order. These three things are used to find the correct entry in the pricing procedure determination table. Typically, within a given sales area, there aren't many pricing procedures. After a material is entered in the sales order line item, the system starts running through the pricing procedure to find the right prices. It does this sequentially, stopping at each condition type in the pricing procedure to see if it gets a hit. For example, if we were selling a bike in our US sales organization, the system would determine our US pricing procedure. It would then check through each condition type to search for a record. If it finds a value, it returns that value to the sales order and shows it on the sales pricing screen, called the CONDITIONS tab (see Figure 4.37).

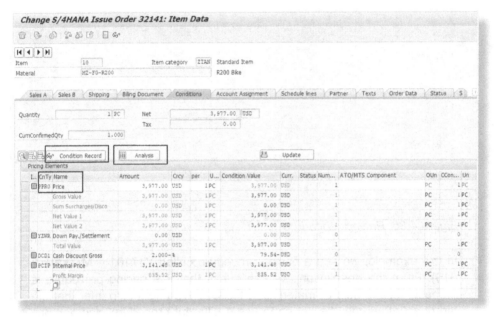

*Figure 4.37: Sales order Conditions tab*

The screenshot shows how the system calculated the price of $3,977.00 for our bike. What we see here is the list of active prices that were found and that are relevant to this item. Some of the prices (condition types) shown here do not impact the net price to the customer. For example, CASH DISCOUNT GROSS and INTERNAL PRICE (cost) are just informational. The condition type of most interest in this example is PPRO, the PRICE, because that is where the net value comes from. Under the PRICE (PPRO) condition type, but not shown on this screenshot, is a sequence of pricing tables (the access sequence). The tables are ordered in a sequence of most specific to least specific because once the system finds a record, it stops the search within that condition type and moves on.

By clicking on the ANALYSIS button we can open up even more pricing details (see Figure 4.38).

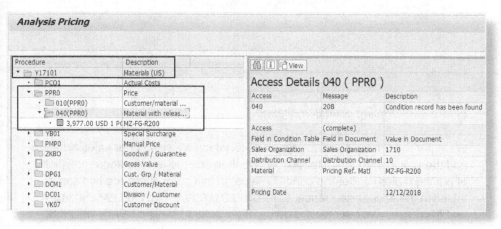

*Figure 4.38: Pricing analysis details*

The screen contains a folder structure on the left, where the top level is the pricing procedure (in this case Y17101). Under that, there are folders for each condition type. Under the condition types, are folders for each level of the access sequence; these are sometimes referred to as *key combinations*. If we look at PPR0, we can see two folders: 010 – CUSTOMER/ MATERIAL, and 040 – MATERIAL WITH RELEASE. Under the second folder, we can see a value of 3,977.00 USD. This tells us that the pricing record was found here. The system first searched to see if there was a specific price set for the combination of this customer and this material. When it didn't find one, it moved on to the next search level, looking for a record with just that material. The right side of the screen gives us even more detail, showing that the sales area and the date (prices always have validity dates) were also taken into account.

Having found a value for PPR0, the system moves down the list and checks the next condition type; here, YB01 – SPECIAL SURCHARGE. In this case, nothing is found, so it keeps moving down the list.

Another way to both see and maintain the prices that have been set up is via pricing condition change (see Figure 4.39).

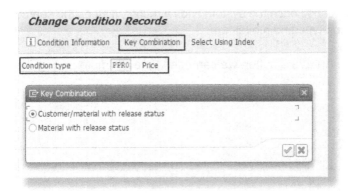

*Figure 4.39: Pricing condition change*

We enter the pricing condition type *PPR0*, which we saw in our sales order, and then click on KEY COMBINATION. We then see the access sequence (list of pricing tables) under the condition type. In this case, there are two steps/ tables in the access sequence: CUSTOMER/MATERIAL WITH RELEASE STATUS and MATERIAL WITH RELEASE STATUS. If we select MATERIAL WITH RELEASE STATUS, we see the same price that we saw on our sales order (see Figure 4.40).

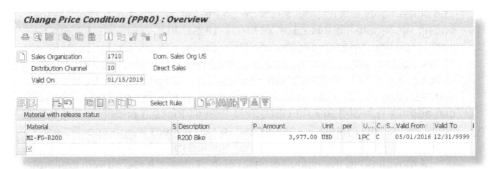

*Figure 4.40: Pricing condition record*

We can see that this price is valid for our sales area and for our bike material. We also see the price in USD (US dollars), per unit of measure (PC), and the validity dates from 05/01/2016 to 12/31/9999 (that's a long time!).

If we were to create another pricing record at the customer/material level, what do you think would happen in the sales order? Great question! Like so many things in SAP, the answer is: it depends. As you can see in Figure 4.41 we now have two pricing condition records.

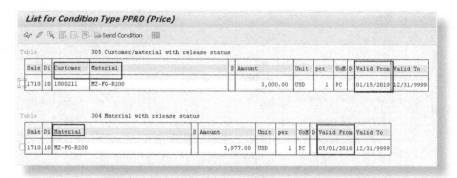

Figure 4.41: Two pricing condition records

If we were to go back and add this material again to the order we previously created, nothing would change. That's because, looking at Figure 4.42, we see that the order has a PRICING DATE that is earlier than our VALID FROM date on our newly-created condition record, which starts on 01/15/2019.

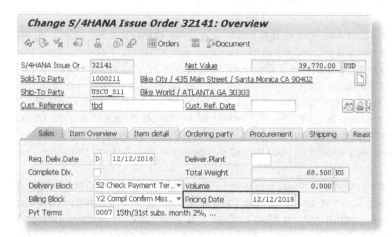

Figure 4.42: Order pricing date

The PRICING DATE on the order defaults from the order creation date, but this can be changed manually. If we change the order pricing date to be 01/15/2019, then our new CUSTOMER/MATERIAL pricing record gets pulled into the order because it comes first in the access sequence; it is more specific than just MATERIAL (see Figure 4.43).

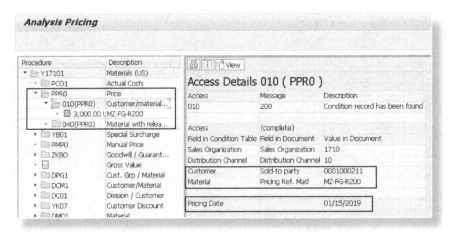

Figure 4.43: New pricing

As you can see in the screenshot, the CUSTOMER/MATERIAL record now shows the new PRICING DATE of 01/15/2019.

Once the system has found the price, it moves down the list of condition types in the pricing procedure and searches for a match. For example, the next condition type may be a discount. If a discount record is found, it appears with a value in the conditions tab of the sales order, and reduces the net value. There might also be other condition records, such as a surcharge, or freight, or sales tax. Finally, the result of all these prices is added up to obtain different sub-totals and totals. There is, of course, a lot more functionality and flexibility available, but this is the general idea behind pricing.

"Phew!", said Lauren, rubbing her eyes. Ok, pricing is master data, and the condition technique is used to find the right prices. There seems to be a lot of flexibility with it, which also makes it a little hard to wrap your head around. No wonder she couldn't find the price on the material master. The prices lived elsewhere, in condition records in pricing tables.

## Top-down pricing

Pricing in SAP works top down in that you generally start with a base price and then apply discounts and surcharges. Along the way, there can be additional pricing condition types for sales tax, and statistical prices for reporting. Pricing is also tied in with finance and controlling, and can influence which general ledger (G/L) accounts are posted to during billing.

# 5 Sales order processing

**In this chapter, we continue our examination of some of the primary functions of the sales order, including item categories, availability checking, dates, shipping, texts, and more.**

After coming to terms with all of that master data, Lauren was ready to continue with her learning. She opened her training manual to the sales order chapter, and read on.

## 5.1 The item category

The most fundamental control element in the OTC process is the sales order *item category* (see Figure 5.1).

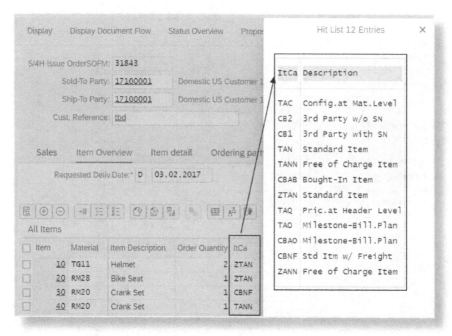

*Figure 5.1: Item category*

Every sales order line item has an item category that tells the system how to behave. The item category controls just about everything that happens in the sales process, and flows through the sales order, the delivery, and the billing document. While the sales order type is influential, it is really the mighty item category that sets the direction of most SD processes. In fact, one of the major functionalities of the sales order type is to help determine the item category, so the two are very closely linked. The item category even tells the system which schedule line category to use. Let's take a look at what the item category does. Behind the scenes, each item category is configured to behave in a certain way. Let's now examine the configuration settings within the standard out-of-the-box item category TAN (see Figure 5.2).

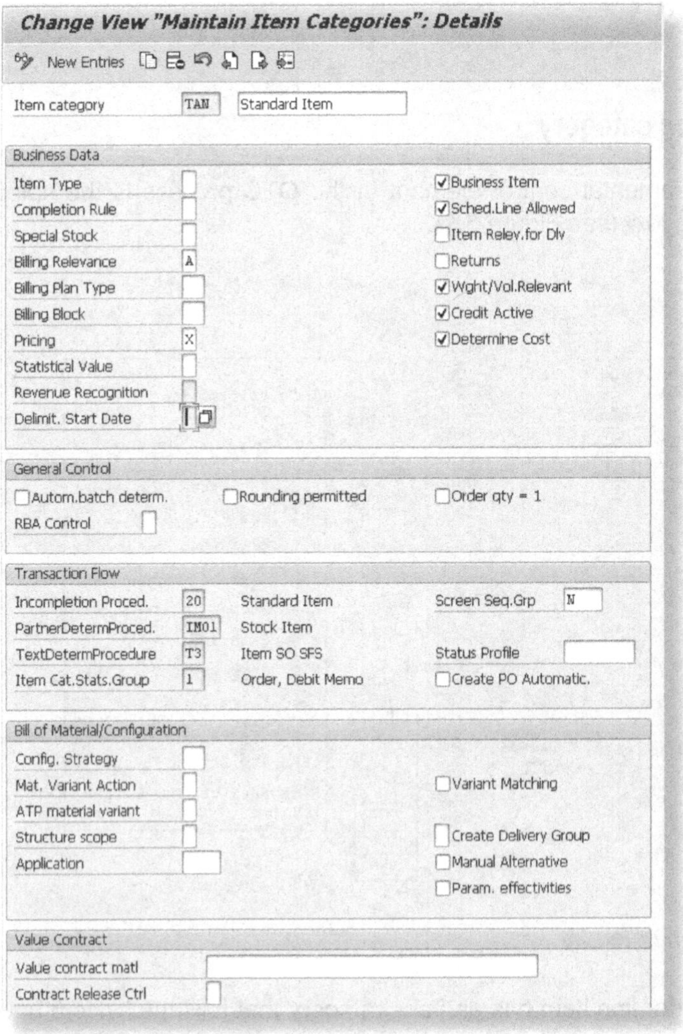

*Figure 5.2: Item category TAN settings*

As you can see, there are many fields here and each one controls how the item category behaves (even the blank entries have a meaning). We'll look closely at a part of the configuration, and compare the settings between a STANDARD ITEM category and a SERVICE ITEM category (see Figure 5.3).

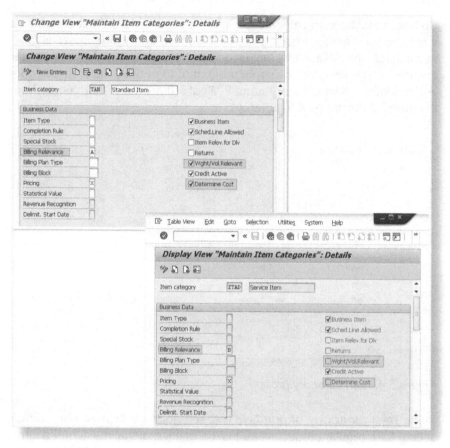

*Figure 5.3: Item category settings compared*

You'll notice that the first difference between the two item category settings is the BILLING RELEVANCE setting: A for a standard item, and B for a service item. A means delivery-related billing (i.e., billing from a delivery document), and B means order-related billing. This makes sense, because a service is not a physical product and it doesn't involve a delivery. In the PRICING field, we see an X for both. That's because both products and services are relevant for pricing. However, in the WGHT/VOL.RELEVANT checkbox we see another difference—the service item is not selected. That's because, logically, a service doesn't have a weight (maybe a wait, but definitely not a weight). It's important to understand that it's not the item-category letters (TAN or ZTAD) themselves that are coded into the system and control the behavior, it's the settings under the item category that tell the system what to do.

So how does the item category get into the sales order? What determines that? Glad you asked! In fact, there is an *item category determination table* that controls this. Within that table, you'll find the combination of sales order document type and *item category group* that then drive the item category determination. Item category group? What's that? Well, that comes from the material master (see Figure 5.4).

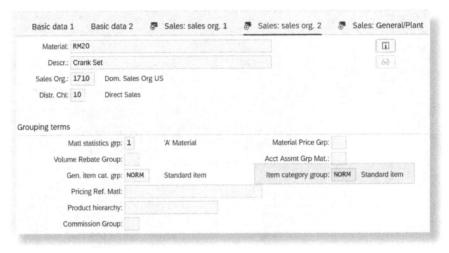

*Figure 5.4: Item category group*

In the ITEM CATEGORY GROUP field, we see good old NORM, our 'normal' setting for a regular product. If we looked at the material master for a service product, we would see it has an item category group of LEIS (service without delivery) or DIEN (service with delivery). The way it works is that the system takes the sales order type and the item category group from the material master, and then plugs them into the item category determination table to find the right item category, which it then pops into the sales order line as soon as you press ⌷Enter⌷. The result is shown in Figure 5.5.

**Change View "Item Category Assignment": Overview**

New Entries

| SaTy | ItCGr | Usg. | HLevItCa | DfItC | MItCa | MItCa | MItCa |
|------|-------|------|----------|-------|-------|-------|-------|
| OR | LEER | | TAN | TAZ | | | |
| OR | LEIK | | | PO | POLL | | |
| OR | LUMB | | | TAPB | | | |
| OR | LUMB | | TAPB | TAN | | | |
| OR | NORM | | | TAN | | TAQ | TANN |
| OR | NORM | | TAG | TAN | | | |
| OR | NORM | | TAN | TANN | | | |
| OR | NORM | FREE | TAN | TANN | | | |

*Figure 5.5: Item category determination table*

The table also enables you to control which item categories can be manually selected by the user. In the example shown, the user could also select TAQ or TANN as item categories.

## 5.2 Availability checking

Lauren knew that in addition to pricing, the other thing that customer's always cared about was when they were going to get their goods. She turned to the training manual once again.

One of the key benefits of SAP's built-in integration is the *available-to-promise (ATP)* functionality. In the sales order, this allows us to tell the customer when their products will be available. ATP is based on a set of configured rules about what to consider when promising a product. These rules are contained within the *scope of check* (see Figure 5.6).

Figure 5.6: ATP Scope of Check

It's easiest to understand the scope of check rules through an example. Let's say we create a sales order line item for 100 of our MZ-FG-R200 bikes. The rules within the availability check control how many of those bikes can be confirmed as available for this sales order, and on which dates. If there are currently only 88 of these bikes in inventory, what should we do? Should we promise only 88 bikes? Or should we look beyond what is currently in stock and consider all the open production orders and open purchase orders, and then let the system calculate when we can promise the remaining 12 bikes? Or, should we have a *replenishment lead time*, which is a default amount of time that we know it takes to build or procure the items? All of these types of rules are contained within the scope of check, and the results are shown on our sales order SCHEDULE LINES (see Figure 5.7).

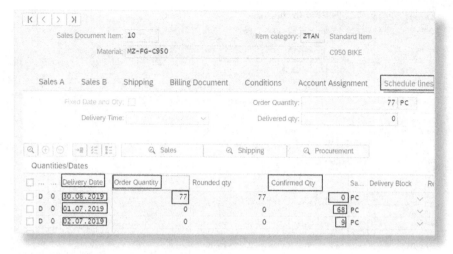

*Figure 5.7: Sales order Schedule lines*

In the screenshot, we can see the delivery dates and the confirmed quanti-ties for each date. The order was for 77 bikes for June 30, and the system was able to confirm 68 for July 1, and 9 for July 2 (shown here in European date format).

So how does this work in daily life? Figure 5.8 shows that when a sales order is created, the REQ. DELIV.DATE (required delivery date) field defaults to the current date. This is the date we want the product, usually as soon as possible. The user can change this date to a future date, if so desired. This header-level required date is then copied to all the line items in the FIRST DATE column, which tells the system the date we want each line item. Each line item can have different required dates, if needed.

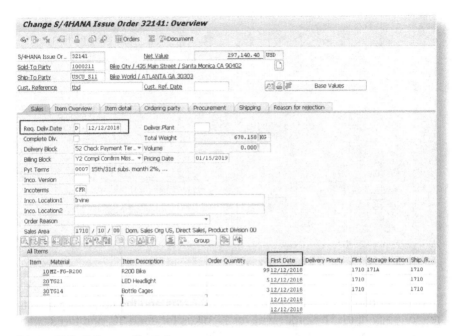

*Figure 5.8: Sales order dates*

Under each sales order line item are the schedule lines, which are found on the SCHEDULE LINES tab in the ITEM DATA screen (see Figure 5.9).

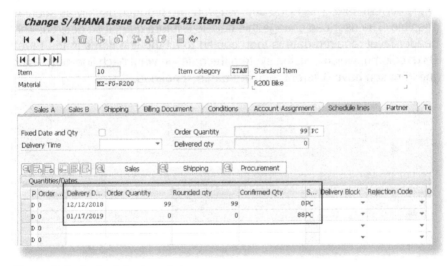

*Figure 5.9 : Schedule lines tab*

Schedule lines are all about dates and quantities. In the screenshot, we can see that at our sales order ITEM number is 10 and that we are requesting an order quantity of 99 bikes on 12/12/2018. The system returns the next line, saying that it can only confirm 88 bikes on 01/17/2019, and nothing more. Presumably, this is because the scope of check does not include a standard replenishment lead time. This doesn't mean that the requirement for the additional 10 bikes has disappeared. That requirement is still used in the system to decide how many more bikes to build or buy; however, as of right now, there are no plans in the system and we can't promise them to the customer.

When the user first enters their sales order line items, the availability check is triggered. Typically, if all the quantities are not available on the dates requested, the AVAILABILITY CONTROL screen appears, as shown in Figure 5.10, giving the user the opportunity to decide what to do (you can configure whether a screen pops-up or not).

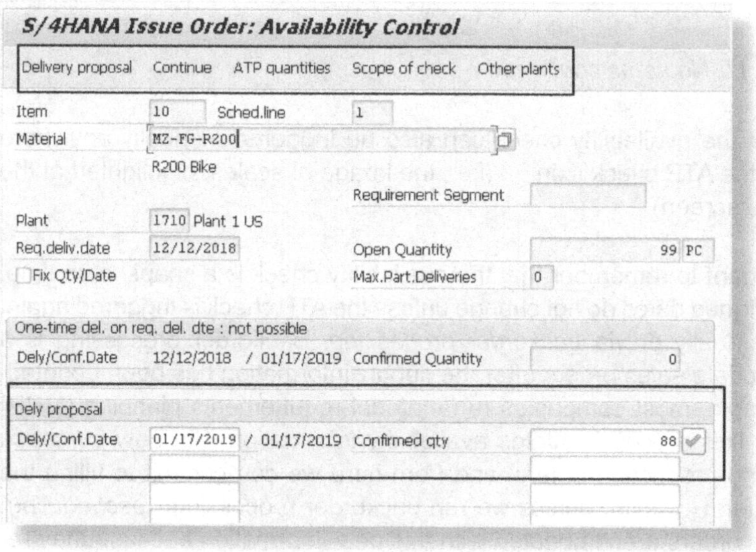

### S/4HANA Issue Order: Availability Control

| Delivery proposal | Continue | ATP quantities | Scope of check | Other plants |
|---|---|---|---|---|

| Item | 10 | Sched.line | 1 | |
|---|---|---|---|---|
| Material | MZ-FG-R200 | | | |
| | R200 Bike | | | |
| | | Requirement Segment | | |
| Plant | 1710 Plant 1 US | | | |
| Req.deliv.date | 12/12/2018 | Open Quantity | | 99 PC |
| Fix Qty/Date | | Max.Part.Deliveries | 0 | |

One-time del. on req. del. dte : not possible

| Dely/Conf.Date | 12/12/2018 / 01/17/2019 | Confirmed Quantity | | 0 |
|---|---|---|---|---|

Dely proposal

| Dely/Conf.Date | 01/17/2019 / 01/17/2019 | Confirmed qty | | 88 ✓ |
|---|---|---|---|---|

*Figure 5.10: Availability Control screen*

The screenshot shows us that we requested a quantity (OPEN QUANTITY) of 99 pieces on 12/12/2018, and that 0 are confirmed for that date. It has a delivery proposal (DELY PROPOSAL) of 88 on 01/17/2019. It is now up to the user to either agree to the delivery proposal, or not. To agree, the user clicks on the green checkbox or on DELIVERY PROPOSAL. If they don't agree to it, they click on CONTINUE. If the proposal is not accepted, then nothing is confirmed, but the demand for the product, also known as a *requirement*, still remains in the system (see Figure 5.11).

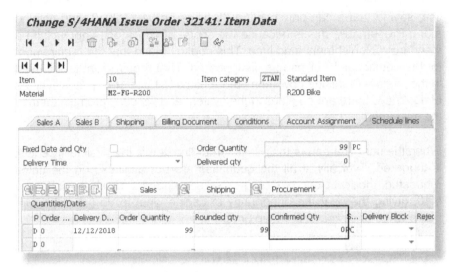

*Figure 5.11: No items confirmed*

Note that the availability check can also be triggered manually anywhere you see the ATP check icon   (i.e., the image of scales, highlighted at the top of the screen).

It's important to remember that the availability check is a snapshot in time. The confirmed dates do not change unless the ATP check is triggered again, either manually or via *backorder processing*. Backorder processing is a way to update sales orders after the supply information has been updated. For example, most companies run material requirements planning (MRP) at night. This process updates availability information with new purchase orders and production orders; and from here we can commit to filling the sales order. However, unless we run backorder processing (*rescheduling*) our sales orders aren't updated with this new information because they remain fixed with the availability promise dates they had when the order was first created. For some businesses, this is the desired state—they don't want the promise dates changing and leading to potential customer aggravation or confusion. Other businesses prefer that the promise dates do change—either to reflect customer priority or to reflect the most updated and/or optimized availability information—and so they run backorder processing on a regular basis.

Now, if we look at the third item on our sales order, where we have ordered some bottle cages, we'll see a different feature of SAP's tight integration (see Figure 5.12).

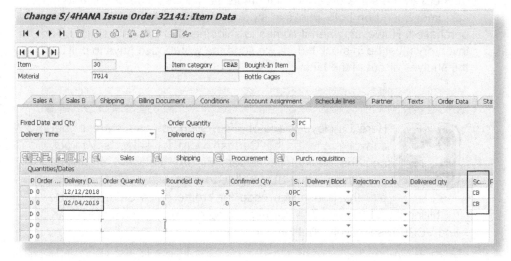

*Figure 5.12: Third-party item*

SAP supports a process called *third-party ordering*. In this scenario, an individual sales order line item can directly create a purchase requisition for the product so that when the customer orders it, we can immediately order it from our vendor. The product can then be drop shipped directly to the customer or sent to our warehouse. In our example, we see that the ITEM CATEGORY is different to our other lines. We also notice that the scope of check for availability is based on our purchasing lead times, rather than what is in inventory. We confirm the date based on how long it takes the vendor to pick, pack, and ship.

## 5.2.1 Schedule lines and deliveries

Schedule lines on the sale order are what drives the creation of deliveries. As we'll discuss in subsequent chapters, the delivery documents control the shipping processes for our order-to-cash flow. The schedule lines are a key integration point between the sales order and the delivery document—they contain the dates and quantities of what we are able to promise to our customers. After all, we wouldn't want to create delivery documents weeks before they are needed. Deliveries are created when they are required, with just enough lead time to pick, pack, and get the products out the door and on the way to our customers. Delivery documents use their own *checking rule* (scope of check) to confirm that the product is actually in inventory, in preparation for shipping. In the standard delivered configuration, the scope of check in the sales order is a little more flexible; we can promise to our customer based on both what's in stock and what's planned to be built or purchased. However, when it comes to shipping, the rule gets stricter. The inventory must be in stock before we send the warehouse guys to pull it off the shelves or out of the bins.

---

**SD and the 'V'**

 Here's a clever piece of information you can impress your co-workers with: the German word for sales is *Verkauf*, and the original developers of SAP software organized everything in the SD module to start with a 'V'. For example, the transaction code for create sales order is VA01, for billing it's VF01, etc. The corresponding database tables are VBAK and VBRK respectively. Welcome to V-land!

---

## 5.3  Working with sales orders

The next day, Lauren was ready to move on. She had learned how schedule lines control the dates and quantities on a sales order, and now she was ready to ship and bill. However, she still needed to clean up a few things on her test order, and she wanted to see how it looked printed out. She opened up her web browser and found her order. One of the things she noticed in the web browser was that when she put her mouse over a field, a short description of it appeared.

In her order, she spotted that her SHIP-TO PARTY was missing a street address (see Figure 5.13).

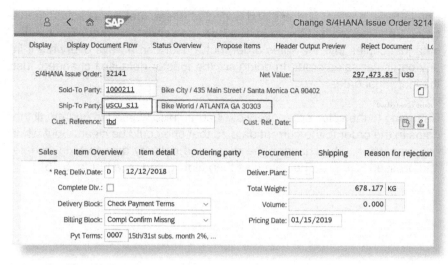

Figure 5.13: Sales order overview

She wondered if she could add the street address directly to the order, or if she needed to update the customer master and then recreate the order over again? Crossing her fingers, she double clicked on the SHIP-TO PARTY in her order and a screen opened where she could enter the street address (see Figure 5.14).

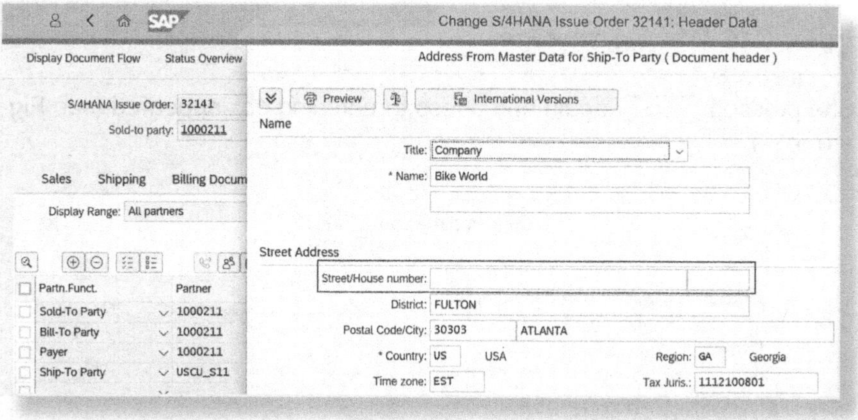

Figure 5.14: Ship-to street address field

She entered a street address and was glad to see that it was saved to the order. She realized that this fit in with how master data worked. The master data just copies into the sales order, but a user can always overwrite it in any particular sales order. In doing so, the master data isn't changed, just the individual order.

Returning to the sales order overview, Lauren also wanted to update all the dates in the order to the current date so that she could be clear about what happens when. She changed the requested delivery date to today's date and pressed [Enter]. The date was then highlighted (see Figure 5.15).

*Figure 5.15: Changed delivery date*

An ominous looking message then appeared at the bottom of her order (see Figure 5.16).

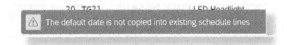

*Figure 5.16: Warning message*

She pressed [Enter] again and a less threatening box appeared (see Figure 5.17).

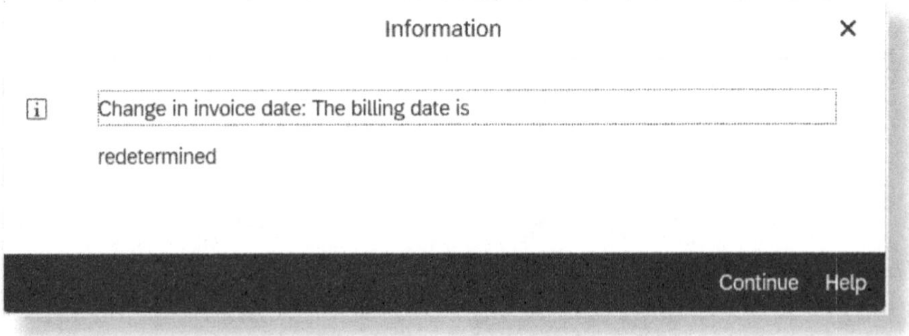

| Information | × |
|---|---|
| ⓘ  Change in invoice date: The billing date is | |

redetermined

Continue    Help

*Figure 5.17: Informational message*

She pressed $\boxed{\text{Enter}}$ one more time, and all the messages went away. She thought about what the messages had stated. The first one had said: THE DEFAULT DATE IS NOT COPIED INTO EXISTING SCHEDULE LINES. She correctly interpreted that as SAP's way of indicating that the new date she entered wasn't going to change the dates on the lines she had previously entered; it would only impact new lines. She could see this in action on her line items. Her existing lines had kept a requested first delivery date of 12/12/2018, whereas the new empty lines had all defaulted to her new date of 01/22/2019 (see Figure 5.18).

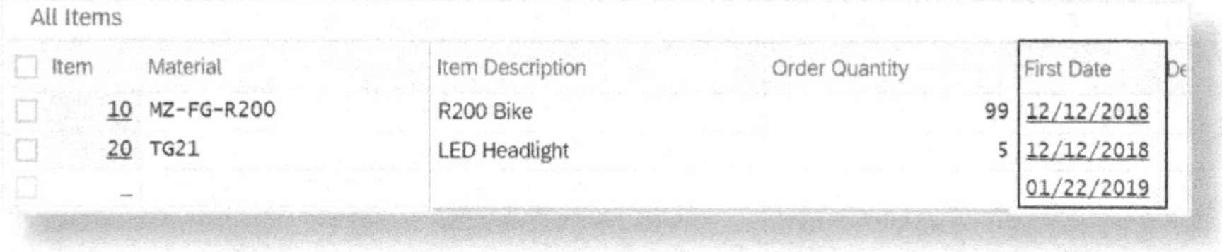

| All Items | | | | | |
|---|---|---|---|---|---|
| ☐ Item | Material | Item Description | Order Quantity | First Date | De |
| ☐ 10 | MZ-FG-R200 | R200 Bike | 99 | 12/12/2018 | |
| ☐ 20 | TG21 | LED Headlight | 5 | 12/12/2018 | |
| ☐ | — | | | 01/22/2019 | |

Figure 5.18: Line item requested dates

She cut and pasted her new date into the other two existing line items and they both changed; with no warning messages this time.

The other message had said: CHANGE IN INVOICE DATE: THE BILLING DATE IS REDETERMINED. Aside from some questionable grammar and strange syntax, that made sense—change the requested date and the billing date changes. But is that different to the invoice date? And what does that do exactly? She decided she'd investigate more once she started billing for the order.

Now that she was getting the hang of things, she decided to explore a few other fields and tabs on the sales order header, before she moved on to billing. On the SALES tab, she saw the ORDER REASON field and recalled from her training that it could be used to drive reporting, as well as trigger pricing and special discounts. She thought that maybe she could use that field to reduce the number of order type choices that the customer service reps sometimes complained about.

On the SHIPPING tab, she saw a number of fields related to shipping, which was familiar to her from past experience (see Figure 5.19).

*Figure 5.19: Order shipping tab*

She knew that companies typically need to indicate how products are going to ship at the time of the order, what it will cost, and how long it will take. She opened her training manual to see what else she could learn.

## 5.3.1 Sales order shipping options

Quite often, there is a need to choose the carrier and the service level to drive shipment times and costs, as well as freight charges. The shipping conditions field is quite flexible and, depending on the business needs, can be used to define when an order will ship, how it will ship, and/or who will ship it. For example, some companies use the field as a combination of carrier and service level, with entries such as UPS Ground, UPS 2nd Day, FedEx Overnight, etc. A different approach is for the shipping condition to simply represent whether it's parcel carrier or truckload shipping, and different fields such as the SPECIAL PROCESSING INDICATOR to represent the service level (2nd day, overnight, etc.). In addition, a third field, a partner function, represents the carrier, such as FedEx. One of the benefits of using the shipping conditions field is that any time the entry is changed, standard SAP prompts the user to do a redetermination of shipping-related calculations, which can be used to recalculate freight prices, routes, and delivery estimates.

## 5.4 Listings and exclusions—members only

We sometimes want to restrict what our customers can purchase. We could have scenarios where we make a special product line specifically for one customer, that nobody else can buy. Or we may have a scenario where a given customer can only buy one type of product. These types of scenarios are handled through SAP's *listing and exclusion* functionality. *Listing* means that a customer can only buy items that are contained within rules set up for that customer. *Exclusion* means that you set up rules to determine goods that the customer cannot buy. This functionality leverages the condition technique that we discussed in the pricing section. In listings and exclusions, we have a procedure, condition types, access sequences, and condition records, just as with pricing, so it is very flexible.

Let's look at an example of an exclusion, which is far more common than a listing. At Brand X, we have a scenario where only our premium bike shops can sell our high-end bike models. No other customers are allowed to buy these bikes from us, so we set up an exclusion to support this. We have an exclusion condition type, with a key combination of customer group (the type of customer) and material group (premium bikes). We enter the condition record for the combination of all customer groups, except premium customer, and the material group for premium bikes. The result is that when a sales order is created, the system retrieves the customer group the customer belongs to, and the material group the material belongs to. It then searches for any exclusion records for this combination, and if it finds one, a message appears stating that 'the material is excluded', thus preventing the sale of that item.

On the other hand, listings allow a customer to buy only what they are listed for. For example, at Brand X we make private label bikes for a big customer. We set up a listing with the combination of that customer number, and a material group for those private label bikes. This means that if that customer ever tries to buy something that doesn't belong to that private label bike category, the system will not allow it. Note that having a listing doesn't exclude other customers from buying that product, it is just a 'list' of what a particular customer can buy.

## 5.5 BOMs away—sales BOMs

A *BOM (Bill of Material)* is a structured grouping of materials, typically hierarchical. BOMs are used across different functional areas and, as a result, there are different categories of BOMs in SAP. For example, a production BOM for a bicycle might be structured something like this:

- ▶ 1234 Mountain Bike
  - ▶ 43145 Frame Qty 1
  - ▶ 52433 Fork Qty 1
  - ▶ 75884 Wheel Qty 2

Under each of the second level items, there could be another hierarchy of all the material components that are used to build them. For example, a wheel might consist of a rim, spoke, bearings, etc. The production BOM defines what parts are needed to build a given product.

On the sales side, we've got our own BOMs, not surprisingly called *sales BOMs*. Sales BOMs relate to the selling and shipping of products, and not to how they are built. A classic use of sales BOMs is what is sometimes referred to as *bundling,* or *sales kits*. For example, a laptop bundle might include a laptop, a mouse, and office software. A special material number is created to represent the bundle (the top-level material of the sales BOM). Then, the sales BOM itself is created, joining the top level with the components and quantities that make up the bundle (i.e., the laptop, mouse, and software). When the sales BOM is entered into a sales order, it *explodes* (yes, that's what it's called!) into its component parts so that you can see what it consists of. One of the key features of sales BOMs is that, by default, the system makes sure that all the components ship together, using the delivery group indicator. Like all things SAP, there are different configurable options available with sales BOMs. There are two flavors of BOMs which are affectionately, yet awkwardly, known as LUMF and ERLA because of their item category groups. They are all about availability and pricing. Do you want to price at the header level or component level? In other words, do you set a price for the laptop bundle itself? Or, do you roll up the price of each individual component of the sales BOM? Same thing for availability checking. Do we check the availability of the top-level item or the components? Not surprisingly, the two different flavors of sales BOMs lead to two different item categories in the sales order line which control the behavior of pricing and ATP. It can also be configured so that one of the component items is free (i.e., buy a laptop, and get a free office software bundle). This leads us right into the next topic....

## 5.6 Free goods

When it comes to giving away products for free, there are as many different flavors as there are hot sauce. There are BOGOs (buy one, get one free), samples, bundles, promotions, and spiffs. Let's break it down to understand what the options are in SAP. We'll start with the order type *CBFD (free-of-charge delivery)*. This order type makes use of a 100% discount pricing condition that is automatically triggered based on the order type itself. On these orders, whatever price the product has is automatically discounted. The discounted amount can be posted to a special G/L account so that finance can keep track of the discounts; and not just see zero revenue and wonder why profit margins are shrinking.

Another free option we have is the ability to change the item category on a sales order to be a free one, thereby deactivating pricing for the line item and ignoring the product value. Finance might then wonder why profit margins are shrinking. So why we would want to change the item category rather than just changing the price to zero? Glad you asked! There are several reasons, but the most important one is that, by default, regular item categories require a net value. If the value is zero, the sales order line is incomplete. Why, you ask? Well, it's a fail-safe so that if the system doesn't find a price, we don't ship goods out for free. That would be awkward to explain to your boss, wouldn't it?

It's worth noting that neither of the above two free scenarios change the cost posting. The cost of goods still posts to the regular cost-of-goods (COGS) account upon post goods issue (PGI). Sometimes, the finance folks have other ideas for a free scenario and want a different type of cost posting. The good news (for them) is that through a little fancy configuration of item categories, schedule line categories, and more, we can control these postings.

But wait, there's more free stuff! SAP has special functionality for what it calls *free goods*, and what the internet calls BOGO. SAP uses the condition technique to set up and manage these offers. As a result, there is plenty of flexibility in setting up the rules for free-goods processing, which can actually be more complex than you might think. Because sales and marketing folks skew towards being more creative, they come up with all kinds of offers we have to figure out how to support. Do all customers get the free item or just some? The condition technique allows you to set the rules flexibly regarding who gets what. For example, an offer might be 'buy ten, get one free' for A-list customers buying product X. But does that mean they get charged for nine, and the tenth one is free? Or, is the eleventh item sent for free if they buy ten? SAP manages this with two types of free goods, called *inclusive* and *exclusive*, which handle just such scenarios. And what about the line item? How can a line item be entered for a quantity of ten, but only one of them is free in the extended price? Thankfully, this is all managed by SAP free goods, which automatically creates a new line item for the free item(s), using the free item category.

## 5.7    Material substitution and CMIRs

Sometimes, we just can't get customers to order the way we want them to. They might order last years' parts numbers or insist on using their own parts numbers for our products. Because these types of problems have been around for a long time, SAP has a couple of handy solutions to address them. Let's consider a scenario where a customer orders last year's part number. SAP addresses this issue with a field on the material master called the *cross-chain distribution status*. With this field, we can determine whether a material is available for sales, is discontinued, is allowed only for returns, etc. For example, if a sales person enters a material in a sales order that is marked as returns only, the system issues a message and stops the order. However, if they enter the same material on a return order, they are allowed to proceed. But what about scenarios where last year's part number has been replaced with this year's version of the same thing? Wouldn't it be nice if we could just switch out the old part number for the new? Yes, it would! And that's where *material substitution* comes into play. Material substitution uses the condition technique to set up rules for how to switch one material for another. First, input product X on a sales order line item, then press $\boxed{\texttt{Enter}}$; product Y then magically appears in its place.

The other scenario is where a customer keeps their own numbering scheme for our parts numbers. This is where the *customer material info record (CMIR)* can be used. The CMIR enables us to create a data record for a given customer that maps our part number to their part number. That way, we have both the material numbers on all sales documents for that customer. We can use them during the ordering process and can print them on customer documents such as packing lists and invoices.

## 5.8    Credit checks and credit cards

Continuing her explorations, Lauren noticed a tab called ELECTRONIC PAYMENT. This got her wondering: before we sell products to a customer, how can we ensure they will pay? She opened her manual to the credit chapter, and read on.

## 5.8.1 Credit management

Our company, Brand X, has a wide variety of customers, from small local bike shops to big international distributors, all with varying financial stability. This represents a range of risks to our company. In order to control our risk exposure, we can use SAP's integrated credit management. We assign each customer to a risk category, extend a credit limit, and then the system monitors our credit exposure by tracking the value of sales orders, deliveries, billing documents, outstanding balances, and the payment history for each customer. Each sales order goes through a series of checks based on the rules the finance department has set up in the system. Depending on the situation, a credit block may be triggered at any point during the order-to-cash process. When a credit block is triggered on a sales order, a message appears, indicating that the order is on credit hold (see Figure 5.20).

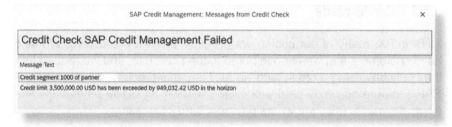

*Figure 5.20: Credit check*

The message typically indicates why the credit check failed, and how much the customer has exceeded their credit limit by. The credit department then uses their own lists to manage sales orders that are on credit hold, They review the customers' credit situations, and release the orders that they choose to.

From the OTC perspective, there are a few points related to credit that are worthy of attention. The first is that a user can tell if a particular sales order has gone on credit hold by looking at the order header STATUS tab. In the OVERALL BLKD STATUS field, a BLOCKED status indicates that the order is blocked, and the OVERALLCREDSTAT field tells us whether the credit hold has been RELEASED or NOT APPROVED (see Figure 5.21).

Processing Status

| | |
|---|---|
| Overall Status: | In Process |
| Rejection Status: | Nothing Rejected |
| Delivery Status: | Not Delivered |
| OverallCredStat: | Not Approved |
| Overall Blkd Status: | Blocked |
| System status: | REL |

*Figure 5.21: Credit status*

The second feature to note is that when an order goes on credit hold, the standard setting is for all schedule line items to be unconfirmed, and the demand requirements are not passed over to purchasing or production. This means that if an order goes on credit hold, we don't start building it or buying for it. Note that this setting is configurable and some industries might choose to take a different approach.

## 5.8.2 Credit cards

At Brand X, many of our customers prefer to pay via credit card. We also have customers that we choose not to extend credit to, and we require that they only buy using a credit card. To facilitate this process, we make use of SAP's integrated credit card processing, known as *digital payments/electronic payments* (also known as *payment card processing*).

The sales order has an ELECTRONIC PAYMENTS tab (also called PAYMENT CARDS tab, depending on the release) where one can enter the customer's credit card details such as the card type, card number, and expiration date (see Figure 5.22).

| Sales | Shipping | Billing Document | Electronic Payments | Billing plan | Accounting | Conditions | Account Assignment | Partner | Texts | Ord... |
|---|---|---|---|---|---|---|---|---|---|---|

| | | | |
|---|---|---|---|
| Authorized | 0.00 | Total | 970.21 USD |
| NextDlv/Se | 894.20 | Next date | 12/10/2019 |

Status of last authorization

| | | | |
|---|---|---|---|
| Requirement Sts | Not Relevant | Authorization Block | |
| Call Status | Not Relevant | | |
| Response | Not Relevant | | |

| | Manual authorization | | Settled in billing docs | | Authorization Log |
|---|---|---|---|---|---|

Electronic Payments

| Type | Card Number / Transac... | Valid to | CVV | CVV Usage Status | CVV Check | Payer Name | Maximum amount | Limit to | Status | Authorized Amt | Bl... |
|---|---|---|---|---|---|---|---|---|---|---|---|
| VISA | 4111111111111111 | 12/2022 | 123 | | | | | | | | |

*Figure 5.22: Electronic Payments*

SAP does some simple checks to make sure the card type and card number match, and are valid (e.g., Visa cards start with 4 and have 16 digits, etc.), and that the expiration date hasn't passed. When the order is saved, the system makes an authorization request to a payment gateway, which checks whether the customer has sufficient credit available on their card. It then places an authorization hold for that amount on the customer's card. If the request is successful, the authorization details are returned to the sales order. If the request fails, then the order is blocked for further processing, and a different credit card can be requested from the customer. In order to achieve PCI (Payment Card Industry) compliance, the card number is often *tokenized* (replaced with a different scrambled number) and not stored in our systems. The token serves as a link to retrieve the actual card number, which is stored by an external payment processing partner.

Because authorizations have a shelf life, it is important to understand that the system tries to obtain them at the right time, soon before the product is scheduled to ship. If we obtain the authorization too early, there is a risk that the authorization will expire before payment is collected, and could hold the customer's credit too early. In order to facilitate the correct timing, SAP looks at the schedule line dates to trigger the authorization requests. If we have a sales order with two line items, one shipping tomorrow and one in two weeks, the authorization request is only made for the first line item value when the order is saved. The order needs to be re-authorized as we move closer to the second shipment.

After the order is shipped and billed, the customer's accounts receivable (A/R) balance is automatically cleared. The funds can then be collected from the customer's credit card via a finance process called *settlement*, which is when all the credit card charges for the day are sent to the bank to actually charge the customer's credit card.

### 5.8.3 Texts

Moving along with her sales order, Lauren stopped to look at the TEXTS tab (see Figure 5.23), where she was glad to see that a variety of different notes could be entered: some notes for the customer, some internal, and some specific to different functions such as shipping or billing. She also saw that even very large blocks of text could be cut and pasted or uploaded using the various icons.

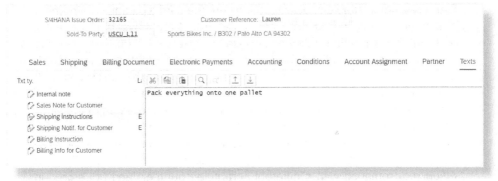

*Figure 5.23: Sales order header texts*

She also remembered that text was available at both header and item level, and could automatically be copied in from the customer or material master. She had also been told that the system could control which text printed out on forms such as the delivery document or customer invoice, via *output*.

## 5.9 Output

In the land of SAP, printed SD documents are called *output*. The reasoning behind this strange name is that printed documents are part of a larger category of things that can be generated or 'output' by SD documents. In addition to printed documents, other things that can be output include EDI messages, email, workflows, etc. From that perspective, perhaps it makes sense that print is just one of several types of output. If it doesn't make sense, don't worry—apparently it didn't make sense to the folks who built the Materials Management (MM) module. They call their output *messages*. Maybe the developers weren't talking that day in Waldorf, Germany? Who knows?

Typically, output is set up to be automated, so that the right outputs come from the right documents, according to a company's business rules. In the pre-HANA world, output is set up via the condition technique. There is an output procedure that is assigned to document types. The procedure then has output condition types (order confirmation, delivery note, invoice, etc.) and master data is created for each one. Each condition type has a print form assigned to it (if relevant). These days, those forms are usually output as PDF documents. Programmers build the forms according to business requirements to pull in whatever fields are needed, in the desired format. With SAP S/4HANA, you have the choice of setting up output the old way, via the condition technique, or the new and improved way, via the Business Rules Framework (BRF+), which is another configurable way of creating business rules in the system. For an end user, it really doesn't matter much. Output allows you to determine when and where the documents are printed out or sent. For example, you can have documents print to your local printer as you save each one, or you may want to have all invoices print at a scheduled time, to a special printer, in the accounting department. All that, and more, is easy to do with output processing.

Lauren stopped reading and went back to her sales order, searching for output. She found a promising menu path: EXTRAS • OUTPUT • HEADER • EDIT (see Figure 5.24 and Figure 5.25).

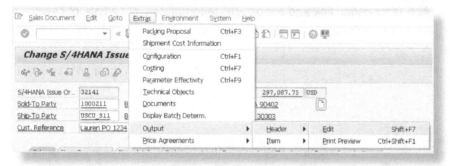

*Figure 5.24: Output in sales order path*

### Change S/4HANA Issue Order 32141: Output

S/4HANA Issue Order 0000032141 ( Edit )

Output

| ID | Status | D... | Output Type | R.. Receiver | Channel | Coun... | Lang... | Form Template |
|----|--------|------|-------------|--------------|---------|---------|---------|---------------|
| 1 | In Preparation | 1 | ORDER_CONFIRMATION | | PRINT | US | EN | SD_SLS_ORDER_CONFIRM |
| 2 | In Preparation | 1 | ORDER_CONFIRMATION | | EMAIL | US | EN | SD_SLS_ORDER_CONFIRM |

*Figure 5.25: Output*

Lauren saw that she could select the PDF icon      and the order confirmation form popped up.

With her order confirmation now in hand, Lauren was ready to move on. Time to ship some product!

## IDOCS

 If you spend a lot of time in the SAP world, one term you're sure to hear is *IDoc*. This does not refer to your local ophthalmologist, but is rather an acronym for the exciting phrase *intermediate document* (although few know why).

An IDoc is a data container, which is a structured way of passing data from one computer system to another. For example, the orders IDoc contains all the sales order fields and information, predefined in a way that shows what belongs to the header level, the line item level, etc. IDocs are commonly generated via....output! And when two SAP systems hook up and start sending IDocs to each other, it's over a nice *ALE (application link and enabling)*—unfortunately not a type of beer!

# 6 Deliveries

**In this chapter, we discuss the process of shipping products, known as delivery processing.**

Lauren was ready to ship products. Preferring to learn by doing, she started exploring her sales order to see if she could figure out how to do it. She came across a menu path that looked promising. Under SALES DOCUMENT, she selected DELIVER, and then a new screen appeared (see Figure 6.1).

*Figure 6.1: Sales order blocked*

She saw red lights and a message saying SALES ORDER IS BLOCKED FOR DELIVERY: CHECK PAYMENT TERMS. She went back to her sales order to see if she could find the problem. Scanning her order, she noticed a field called DELIVERY BLOCK, and that the entry in it said CHECK PAYMENT TERMS. That seemed to be the problem (see Figure 6.2).

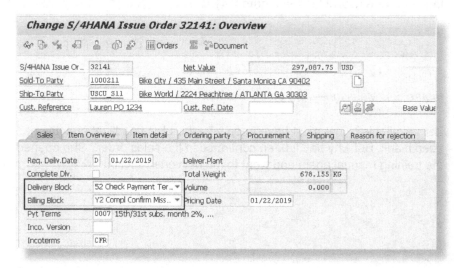

*Figure 6.2: Sales order blocks*

Under DELIVERY BLOCK, she noticed another field called BILLING BLOCK. She decided to remove both of the blocks, and tried again to initiate delivery. This time, she was happy to see that a delivery document screen appeared, showing the products (see Figure 6.3).

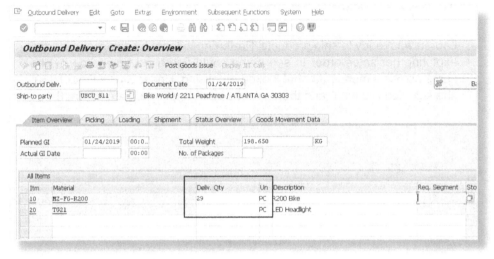

*Figure 6.3: Create delivery document*

The screen showed the SHIP-TO PARTY at the top, and the current date; but something looked wrong. She had ordered 99 bikes on her new sales order, and 5 LED headlights. Why were the delivery quantities different? She typed the number *5* in the delivery quantity field (DELIV. QTY) to see what would happen and a message popped up indicating that no pieces of the item were available (see Figure 6.4).

*Figure 6.4: Message—zero stock available*

Zero available? That must have been why the LED headlight quantity had been blank. But why had it been confirmed in the sales order? She opened the training manual again and went to the deliveries section.

## 6.1 Deliveries—scope of check

As with the sales order, the delivery also does an available-to-promise check. However, in the delivery, we are interested only in what is available in inventory. The scope of check for the delivery only considers what is in inventory and not what is already promised to other orders. That means that it does not consider what is currently being produced or procured. This can sometimes lead to a discrepancy between what has been planned to be available, which could be considered in the sales order, and what is actually physically available in the warehouse, which is what the delivery is concerned with. After all, we can't ship plans—only actual finished products.

Lauren stopped reading. That's it, there must not actually be any of the headlights in inventory. But could she keep going with her test? She pressed SAVE and her delivery was saved with a new number. She selected OUT-BOUND DELIVERY CHANGE from the menu and reviewed her saved delivery (see Figure 6.5).

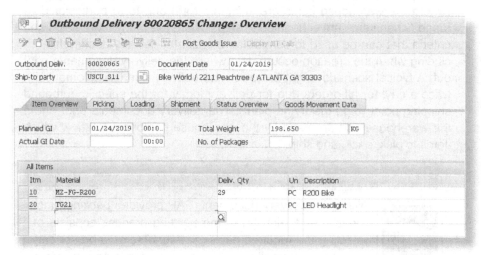

*Figure 6.5: Saved delivery*

So there it was, delivery 80020865—now what?

She decided it best to go back to the manual to get a handle on the delivery process.

## 6.2  Deliveries

The delivery document is the key document for delivering products to customers. Just like sale orders, delivery documents have a header level and an item level. The ship-to party that was on the line item of the sales order appears at the header level of the delivery. The schedule lines that were on the sales order appear at the line item level, and contain the materials and quantities.

A delivery document is a grouping of items that are going to the same place at the same time. Each delivery document has to have one ship-to address and a set of materials that are available to ship on a given date.

Deliveries are typically created in batch mode via the *delivery due list*. A batch program allows the automatic creation of documents.

The delivery due list is typically set up to run for a particular *shipping point* (where the warehouse items are shipping from) and for a particular date range (when items are scheduled to ship). There are many more fields and criteria that can be used to control the creation of delivery documents, including when the creation occurs, and where the delivery documents print out. A typical scenario might be to run the delivery due list automatically, twice a day, for all orders due for delivery today for the specific outbound shipping point (e.g., the Irvine plant). The delivery documents print out in the warehouse and are used by the warehouse personnel to know which items to pick, pack, and ship.

---

**Packing**

 Within the delivery document. SAP provides *packing* functionality. At a high level, the packing process consists of selecting the required *packing material* (e.g., a box or carton), thereby creating a *handling unit* (an auto-generated number that represents the unique box), and then selecting which materials go into which box. If packing rules and master data such as weights and dimensions are set up ahead of time, the packing process can be automated. External shipping systems usually assign a shipping label and a tracking number at the handling unit level because what's in the box doesn't necessarily correspond to the delivery document line items.

---

The information in the sales order is used to drive the delivery process. The confirmed schedule line dates from the sales order tell the system what is ready to be delivered on a given date, and the ship-to party on the sales order line item tells the system where the products are going and how the deliveries should be grouped together. Depending on your system config-uration and business rules, items can be combined across sales orders if they are going to the same ship-to address at the same time, or kept sep-arate. We'll see something similar with billing documents later on.

Once the items are physically picked in the warehouse, the delivery doc-ument is then updated with the actual picked quantities. Depending on your setup, there may be other steps such as *warehouse transfer orders* or *packing,* which are carried out before and after the picking steps in order to move inventory around, and box it up, respectively. Once the picked quantities are updated in the delivery, it's time to send the products to the customer and complete the delivery process. This is done via a step called *post goods issue (PGI)*, where we tell the system that we have shipped the goods out the door. The post goods issue transaction removes the items from our company's inventory and records a cost of goods sold financial transaction. In fact, this is the first time in our OTC process that we make a financial transaction. Nothing in the sales order creates a financial posting until we get to the goods issue step at the delivery stage.

Lauren opened up the delivery screen to see if she could move forward. This time, she clicked on the PICKING tab to see what was there (see Figure 6.6).

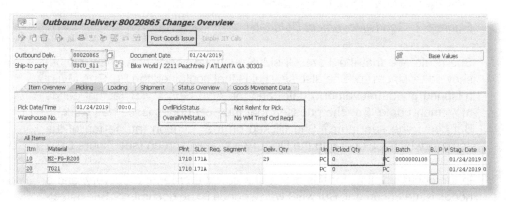

*Figure 6.6: Delivery picking tab*

She noticed that the PICKED QTY (picked quantity) fields were grayed out. She also saw that the overall status said NOT RELVNT FOR PICK. (not relevant for picking), and that no warehouse management (WM) transfer order was required (NO WM TRNSF ORD REQD). She surmised that for some reason this item didn't require picking, so she looked for the next step, POST GOODS ISSUE, which appeared at the top of the screen. She clicked on it to see what would happen.

The wheels turned and she was informed that her delivery was saved. She wondered if anything had happened. Opening up her delivery again, she noticed that the entire document was now gray, which meant she couldn't change anything. That was a good sign, she thought, but how could she find out more? She noticed a GOODS MOVEMENT DATA tab and clicked on it (see Figure 6.7).

*Figure 6.7: Goods Movement Data tab*

She could see that the TOTALGDSMVSTAT (total goods movement status) showed COMPLETED. She also saw fields that contained the PL. GDS MVMT (planned goods movement) date, and the ACT. GDS MVMT (actual goods movement) date. So, she guessed that the post goods issue had worked. But could she see more? She clicked on the      icon (at the top of the screen), which took her into the DOCUMENT FLOW screen (see Figure 6.8).

In the document flow for this order, she saw the order, the delivery, and a goods issue document. But what was a goods issue document? She selected it and clicked on DISPLAY DOCUMENT at the top of the screen.

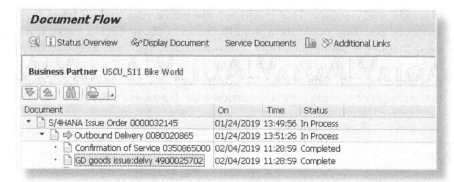

*Figure 6.8: Document Flow screen*

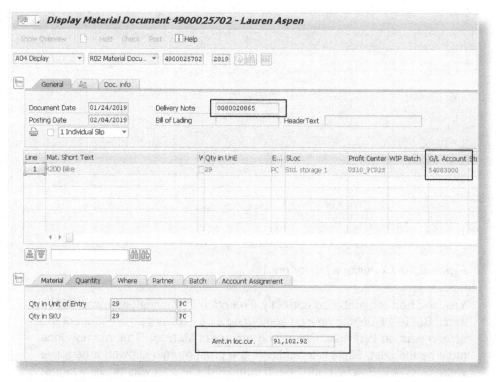

*Figure 6.9: Material Document*

It turned out that the goods issue had created something called a *material document* (see Figure 6.9). She could see her delivery number in it, as well as a G/L ACCOUNT, and an amount of 91,102.92. She looked up that G/L account number and was pleased to see it was the inventory change/cost of goods sold account. That made sense—we've removed 29 bikes from inventory and they would be worth around $91,000, or $3,142 each. However, that didn't seem quite right. From what she recalled, they had been priced to sell to the customer at $3,000 each. Was $3,142 really the cost, or was she confused? She followed the document flow back to her sales order to check. She opened up the CONDITIONS tab (see Figure 6.10).

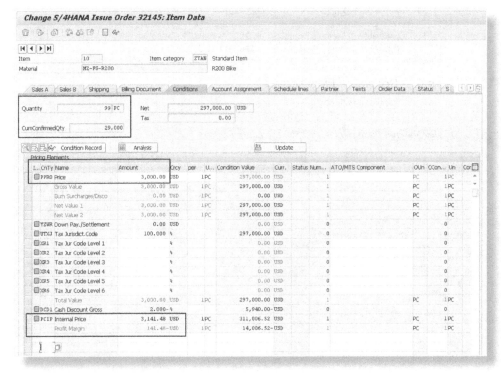

*Figure 6.10: Conditions tab for pricing*

Yes, she had remembered correctly. The price to the customer was $3000 each. But this time she noticed something else—towards the bottom of the screen was an INTERNAL PRICE and a PROFIT MARGIN. The internal price must be the cost, $3,141. In addition, the profit margin showed a negative value of -$141. So she hadn't been confused, the cost was actually higher than the sales price! Yikes! Well, at least there was an easy way to see that. The CUMCONFIRMEDQTY field also told her that only 29 of the 99 bikes she had ordered were confirmed. Good to know. That must have been why the delivery only contained 29, instead of 99, bikes.

Time for lunch, and then on to billing!

## Shipments

 Some companies have the need to manage a group of deliveries. SAP calls this a *shipment* and provides a shipment document to help manage the process. For example, in shipping scenarios that involve loading a truck full of product, there needs to be a way to group all the deliveries that go together. The shipment document can be used to group deliveries together under a common document number, assign output such as a bill of lading, assign a carrier, execute cost estimation, and post an accrual to AP via a *shipment cost document*.

# 7 Billing

In this chapter, we discuss the process of billing and resource-related billing.

## 7.1 Standard billing

Lauren was ready to receive payment for all her effort. She'd ordered, delivered and executed a post goods issue. It was now time to send out the bill! She dove back into the system to see if she could figure it out.

She searched in her delivery document but didn't see anything about billing there, so she searched for billing in her apps, and found several options. She chose the Fiori tile called CREATE BILLING DOCUMENTS – BILLING DUE LIST ITEMS. She clicked on it and was presented with a worklist of documents ready for billing (see Figure 7.1).

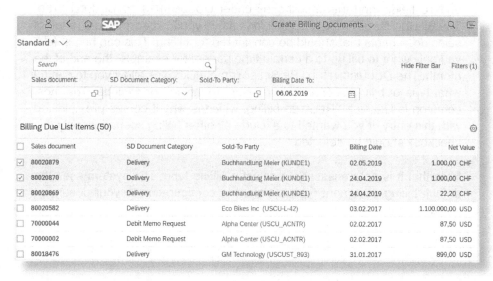

*Figure 7.1: Billing due list*

She saw that she could search, sort, and filter, and then select the documents she wanted to bill. Before she did so, she thought it a good idea to review the manual once again.

Billing is the final step in the order-to-cash process. After we've shipped the goods to the customer, it's time to bill them. In SAP, this is done via a *billing document*. The billing document contains all the details necessary for billing—who gets billed, what gets billed, how much is billed, etc. The billing document is also the foundation of the customer invoice, printed or electronic.

The billing process begins with the creation of the billing document. This is typically done in batch mode via the *billing due list*. As with deliveries, the billing due list can be run manually or via a scheduled batch program. The billing document can also be created individually and directly from a given sales order via a menu path. The MAINTAIN BILLING DUE LIST screen gives users a number of options to determine which documents should be billed (see Figure 7.2).

The different selection criteria in this screen allow you to filter out and create only the billing documents you want to create. For example, you may want to create billing documents just for your sales organization, or for a specific customer. Of particular importance are the BILLING DATE FROM and TO fields, and the checkboxes under DOCUMENTS TO BE SELECTED. The BILLING DATE FROM and TO fields enable you to specify a date range of sales documents that should be considered for billing. This can be useful if you only want to bill up to a certain time period; for example, the end of the month. The DOCUMENTS TO BE SELECTED checkboxes allow you to control what type of billing scenario(s) you want to include or exclude. The most common is DELIVERY-RELATED billing, which is why it comes pre-selected with this entry. If you wanted to exclude all other billing scenarios, only this checkbox should be selected.

Note that it is not necessary to select a billing type. The system uses the default billing document type assigned in configuration to your document types.

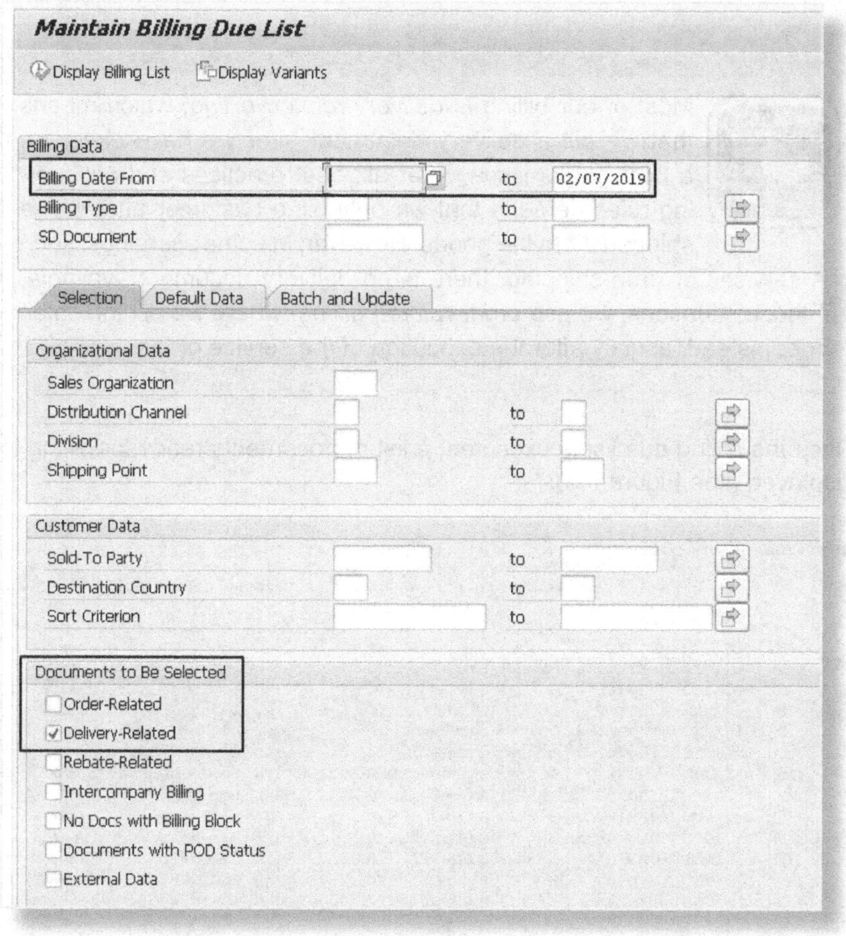

Figure 7.2: Maintain Billing Due List screen

## Order-related billing

Most of our billing is *delivery-related billing*, which means that we bill a delivery document after we have executed a post goods issue. After all, best practices and account-ing rules demand that we only bill a customer after we've shipped them the goods. However, in some scenarios, such as services or drop-shipping, there is no delivery document available. In these situations, we use *order-related billing*, where we bill the sales order instead, usually after the execution of the service or task.

Once the billing due list is executed, a list of documents ready for billing is displayed (see Figure 7.3).

**Maintain Billing Due List**

▲ ▼ 🔍 🔍 📋 ▼ 📋 📋 ▼ 📋 🔲 📊  Individual Billing Document  Collective Billing Document  Collective Billing Doc./Online

| S | BlCat | SOrg. | Billing Date | Sold-to party | BillT | DstC | Document | DChl | Dv | Doc.Cat. | Address | Name of sold-to party | Sold-to locat. | Sort te |
|---|---|---|---|---|---|---|---|---|---|---|---|---|---|---|
| X | L | 1710 | 04/01/2016 | 17100001 | F2 | US | 80003465 | 10 | 00 | J | 23487 | Domestic US Customer 1 | Atlanta | |
| X | L | 1710 | 04/14/2016 | 17100001 | F2 | US | 80003687 | 10 | 00 | J | 23487 | Domestic US Customer 1 | Atlanta | |
| X | L | 1710 | 04/27/2016 | 17100001 | F2 | US | 80003966 | 10 | 00 | J | 23487 | Domestic US Customer 1 | Atlanta | |
| X | L | 1710 | 04/27/2016 | 17100001 | F2 | US | 80003967 | 10 | 00 | J | 23487 | Domestic US Customer 1 | Atlanta | |
| X | L | 1710 | 04/27/2016 | 17100001 | F2 | US | 80003968 | 10 | 00 | J | 23487 | Domestic US Customer 1 | Atlanta | |
| X | L | 1710 | 05/05/2016 | 17100001 | F2 | US | 80003975 | 10 | 00 | J | 23487 | Domestic US Customer 1 | Atlanta | |
| X | L | 1710 | 07/20/2016 | 17100001 | F2 | US | 80007416 | 10 | 00 | J | 23487 | Domestic US Customer 1 | Atlanta | |
| X | L | 1710 | 07/20/2016 | 17100001 | F2 | US | 80007417 | 10 | 00 | J | 23487 | Domestic US Customer 1 | Atlanta | |
| X | L | 1710 | 01/22/2017 | USCU-L-42 | F2 | US | 80018460 | 10 | 00 | J | 28599 | Eco Bikes Inc | RICHMOND | |
| X | L | 1710 | 01/30/2017 | USCU-L-76 | F2 | US | 80018472 | 10 | 00 | J | 31708 | Xeon Bikes Inc | Los Angeles | |
| X | L | 1710 | 01/31/2017 | USCUST_893 | F2 | US | 80018476 | 10 | 00 | J | 31652 | GM Technology | Palo Alto | |
| X | L | 1710 | 02/03/2017 | USCU-L-42 | F2 | US | 80020582 | 10 | 00 | J | 28599 | Eco Bikes Inc | RICHMOND | |
| X | L | 1710 | 02/04/2019 | 1000211 | F2 | US | 80020865 | 10 | 00 | J | 35793 | Bike City | Santa Monica | |

*Figure 7.3: Billing due list*

The list contains information such as the document number that will be billed (in this case delivery documents), the customer, the billing date, etc. All of the list entries come pre-selected for billing, as indicated by the yel-low-highlighted rows and the dark grayed-out buttons on the far left of each row. If we only want to bill some of them we can deselect documents by clicking on the gray boxes for the relevant rows. The remaining yellow-high-lighted rows are the ones that will be billed (see Figure 7.4). Clicking the gray boxes again will re-select those rows for billing.

## Maintain Billing Due List

▲ ▼ 🖨 🖽 ≜ ▽ 🗐 🗋 ▽ ≣ 🎛 🔢  Individual Billing Document  Collective Billing Document  Collective Billing Doc./Online

| S | BlCat | SOrg. | Billing Date | Sold-to party | BillT | DstC | Document | DChl | Dv | Doc.Cat. | Address | Name of sold-to party | Sold-to locat. | S |
|---|---|---|---|---|---|---|---|---|---|---|---|---|---|---|
| X | L | 1710 | 04/01/2016 | 17100001 | F2 | US | 80003465 | 10 | 00 | J | 23487 | Domestic US Customer 1 | Atlanta | |
| X | L | 1710 | 04/14/2016 | 17100001 | F2 | US | 80003687 | 10 | 00 | J | 23487 | Domestic US Customer 1 | Atlanta | |
| X | L | 1710 | 04/27/2016 | 17100001 | F2 | US | 80003966 | 10 | 00 | J | 23487 | Domestic US Customer 1 | Atlanta | |
| X | L | 1710 | 04/27/2016 | 17100001 | F2 | US | 80003967 | 10 | 00 | J | 23487 | Domestic US Customer 1 | Atlanta | |
| X | L | 1710 | 04/27/2016 | 17100001 | F2 | US | 80003968 | 10 | 00 | J | 23487 | Domestic US Customer 1 | Atlanta | |
| X | L | 1710 | 05/05/2016 | 17100001 | F2 | US | 80003975 | 10 | 00 | J | 23487 | Domestic US Customer 1 | Atlanta | |
| X | L | 1710 | 07/20/2016 | 17100001 | F2 | US | 80007416 | 10 | 00 | J | 23487 | Domestic US Customer 1 | Atlanta | |
| X | L | 1710 | 07/20/2016 | 17100001 | F2 | US | 80007417 | 10 | 00 | J | 23487 | Domestic US Customer 1 | Atlanta | |
| X | L | 1710 | 01/22/2017 | USCU-L-42 | F2 | US | 80018460 | 10 | 00 | J | 28599 | Eco Bikes Inc | RICHMOND | |
| X | L | 1710 | 01/30/2017 | USCU-L-76 | F2 | US | 80018472 | 10 | 00 | J | 31708 | Xeon Bikes Inc | Los Angeles | |
| X | L | 1710 | 01/31/2017 | USCUST_893 | F2 | US | 80018476 | 10 | 00 | J | 31652 | GM Technology | Palo Alto | |
| X | L | 1710 | 02/03/2017 | USCU-L-42 | F2 | US | 80020582 | 10 | 00 | J | 28599 | Eco Bikes Inc | RICHMOND | |
| X | L | 1710 | 02/04/2019 | 1000211 | F2 | US | 80020865 | 10 | 00 | J | 35793 | Bike City | Santa Monica | |

*Figure 7.4: Billing due list selection*

In the example above, we have selected some of the deliveries for billing. At this point, we have various options:

▸ click on INDIVIDUAL BILLING DOCUMENT, which creates one billing document for each selected delivery,

▸ click on COLLECTIVE BILLING DOCUMENT, which runs a program in the background and combines deliveries for the same customer into consolidated billing documents (according to business rules), or

▸ click on COLLECTIVE BILLING DOC./ONLINE, which also combines deliveries where appropriate; it does this in the foreground so you can monitor and adjust where needed.

### Combining documents

 Depending on your settings and requirements, SAP has the ability to combine multiple deliveries into a single billing document. In order to do so, the header data must match (i.e., you must be delivering to the same customer, etc.) and you must bill them collectively at the same time. The same applies to sales orders that are billed through order-related billing, and multiple sales orders can combine into a single delivery, if desired.

If the INDIVIDUAL BILLING DOCUMENT is selected, the system shows you the billing document that is about to be created (see Figure 7.5).

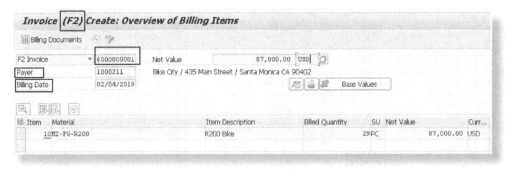

*Figure 7.5: Billing document creation*

There are several important pieces of information on this screen. First, you see F2 included in the title, which refers to the billing document type. As with sales orders and deliveries, there are different document types for billing. Typical examples are *standard invoice* (F2), *credit memo* (G2), and *inter-company* (IV). Based on your system configuration, the correct billing document will be used. Another item of note here is the billing document number (next to the F2 INVOICE field), which is shown here as a placeholder number starting with a squiggly character. After we save the billing document, that number is replaced with the actual billing document number, starting with a 9. The document number ranges can be different per billing document type; for example, regular invoices start with a 9 and credit memos start with a 7. This makes it easy and fast to identify them. Another item of note is the billing document partner, shown on the screen as PAYER; this is the one who pays the bill. It is their account number that gets posted to during the creation of the accounting document. It is their account number that is credit checked. The bill-to information is also found on the billing document, but its importance is limited to where the bill is being sent (postal address or email). Finally, note the BILLING DATE. In delivery-related billing, the billing date defaults from the actual post goods issue date. For order-related billing, it defaults from the billing date field from the sales order. Note that the billing date is not necessarily the same date the billing document was created, although that date (the document date) is also available on the billing document. The billing date is important because it controls the period into which the revenue and receivables are posted.

After creating the billing document, an invoice form can be sent electronically or as a printed document (via output, as discussed earlier). The invoice form is almost always customized with the company's logo and particular

118

formatting requirements. The printing and sending of invoices can be done manually or automatically via a batch program at a time and place of your choosing. For example, some companies choose to run all their billing and printing of invoices overnight, and some choose to print them immediately, when the items ship.

The billing document is an important point of integration with the finance team. The successful creation of a billing document triggers the creation of a corresponding *accounting document.* The accounting document is a financial business document that records the billing entries that are relevant to financial accounting. In the simplest scenario, the accounting document shows a line with a debit to the payer customer's accounts receivable balance (i.e., they owe us money), and with a credit to a sales revenue account (see Figure 7.6).

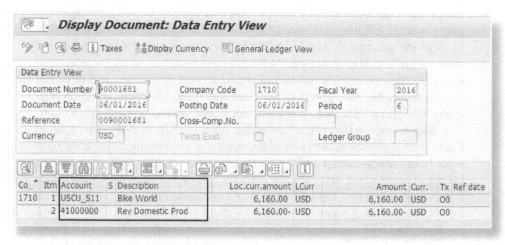

*Figure 7.6: Accounting document*

The particular revenue accounts that are posted to are controlled via an SD configuration step called *revenue account determination.* This can be influenced by the customer, material, pricing, and other factors. It is also fairly typical (although not required) that the billing document and the accounting document have the same number and are kept in synch, which makes for easy investigation and review.

Sometimes, an issue occurs and an accounting document is not created (a billing document does not release to accounting, or there is no journal entry). This can be the result of any number of issues. For example, the accounting period could be closed for a previous month, but your billing document has a billing date from that month. You then have to decide the appropriate course of action—do you open the previous period for posting, or change the billing date to the current month? Thankfully SAP has a tile called MANAGE BILLING DOCUMENTS where you can sort by status, and fix billing documents that have not released to accounting.

Note that the invoice output usually has a routine that checks whether the billing document has released to accounting before printing. This can prevent an awkward situation where a customer gets an invoice for items that have not yet hit the books.

## 7.2  Resource-related billing

So far we've looked at regular billing; i.e., where we bill directly for a product which we have sold to a customer. There are other scenarios where we might want to bill the customer based on the resources that were used to provide the product or service to them. One example of this is *time and materials billing* where we need to bill the customer based on the labor and materials that were used to build or repair a product. In the case of Brand X, we provide bicycle repairs to our customers and bill them based on how many labor hours it took to complete the repair, and what parts were used. To achieve this, we use *resource-related billing* (RRB) in SAP. The repair is tracked on a *service order* (part of the customer service module) where the labor hours are recorded and the parts used are indicated. When it's time to bill the customer, we first execute resource-related billing. Within this function, all the labor and materials costs are converted into billable line items on a special type of sales order called a *debit memo request* (DMR). Once created, the DMR is run through the regular order-related billing process we covered previously. The resource-related billing functionality includes many configuration options that control what and how costs get billed. For example, all the parts used during a repair can be consolidated into one billable line item material called *parts*, or they could each be listed individually. The labor hours could be broken down by type of labor. The RRB process is also commonly used in make-to-order industries, where each product is custom made. For example, imagine building an airplane that is to be sold for 25% more than the cost of the time and materials spent building it. Those costs would most likely be charged to a project in the project systems module, and when ready to bill, resource-related billing would be executed against that project, generating the appropriate DMRs.

## Industry solutions

 SAP is considered a 'packaged' software solution because companies buy it off-the-shelf rather than custom coding their own solution. In addition to the standard SAP software, there is also an option to purchase special industry-specific flavors of the software to suit specific industry needs. For example, there are specific industry solutions for the oil and gas industry, and others for the apparel and footwear industry, all providing functionality specific to those industries. It's still the core SAP software underneath, but additional functionality is added on top to meet particular industry requirements.

# 8 How did we get here?—before the sales order

**In this chapter, we explore two of the major SD pre-sales documents—contracts and quotations.**

Lauren felt that she had a good overview of the order-to-cash process in SD. But she also knew that there was often a lot of work that went into getting a sale, and she wondered if there were any tools in SAP to help with these processes. She opened her manual and read.

## CRM

 *Customer relationship management* (CRM) is of particular interest to us because it crosses over into SD territory. CRM is a set of processes and tools for managing your customer relationships and sales processes. Typical CRM solutions enable a company to manage the entire customer sales lifecycle—from marketing and generating leads, through to tracking sales activities and opportunities, and converting them to quotations and sales orders. Many of the functions in SD are also CRM functions—quotations, sales orders, customer data, pricing, etc. As a result, there is a lot of overlap between SD and CRM. SAP's latest entry into the CRM space is called C/4HANA where they hope to compete directly with large CRM players such as Salesforce.com.

## 8.1 Contracts

Sales contracts in SAP are agreements with the customer to provide products or services, with special terms and/or pricing. Contracts are a special type of sales document and behave similarly to regular sales orders. The distinguishing features of contracts are that they always have a validity period, a date range for which the agreement is valid, and they 'cover' something, meaning that they apply to a particular set of products or dollar values. There are three standard contract types in SD:

1. *Material contracts* apply to a specific material or set of materials. This means that the customer receives the special pricing or terms only when they buy a material covered by their contract.

2. *Value contracts* are agreements with customers to purchase a certain dollar value (or other currency) of products. It can be any material, but they receive the contractual terms only up to a specified dollar limit. Value contracts have the added feature of tracking the amount spent against the target value.

3. *Service contracts* are typically used to manage contractual services. For example, a company could offer a service contract for a particular piece of computer equipment, identified on the contract by serial number. Labor or parts for service or repair could then be covered under the terms of the contract.

We'll now take a look at how a contract works in practice. Let's say a customer enters into an agreement with us to buy $100,000 worth of products over the year. In return for this commitment, we offer them a 10% discount with 'net 180' payment terms. We then create a value contract in SAP to support this. We enter a validity date for the calendar year and a special pricing agreement for the 10% discount. Once the contract is saved, each time an order is placed for this customer a pop-up message appears, indicating that there are open *outline* agreements (SAP's kludgy way of saying there's an open contract) for this customer. It offers to create the sales order *with reference* to the contract, meaning that the data from the first document gets copied into the new one. For example, in this case, the customer, payment terms, and line item details can be copied into the sales order. Not only that, the two documents are now linked in document flow, so you can go to the contract, look at the document flow, and see all the orders that were *called off* against it. In the value contract, you can also see a comparison of the target value (the $100,000) and the value of sales orders created against it.

Let's now look at an example of a service contract. At Brand X, we offer a special deal to bike shops where we service all their bikes every quarter. We sell this service contract to them for $12,000 and with this agreement, all maintenance is 'free'. However, they don't want to pay the full amount upfront, and would rather pay in installments. This is where we would use another common feature in contracts called a *billing plan*. The billing plan enables us to set up the amounts and dates to be billed from the contract. Remember, on a contract we are charging the customer for the agreement and/or services provided and, as such, the billing isn't related to the delivery of a product. In our example, we want to bill the customer $1,000 on the 15th of every month. The billing plan makes it easy to set up these rules and the system then creates billing documents automatically (through order-related billing).

## 8.2  Quotations

A *quotation* is another category of sales document. Like a contract, it is an agreement with the customer to provide goods or services under certain terms. Because it is an agreement, it also has validity dates, which is one of the features that distinguish it from a regular sales order. A quotation is only valid for a certain time period and after that, it expires. Quotations in SAP are quite flexible and, depending on the business needs, can be used as a formal agreement to provide products for an agreed-to price on a certain date, or, more casually, as just a record of a discussion with a customer who was interested in a certain product or service. SAP has another sales document category called *inquiries*, which can be used to do a price and/or availability check for a customer and which can store a record of the customer inquiry. However, the difference between an inquiry and a quotation are minimal, and here at Brand X we only use quotations.

One of the key features of quotations is that they can be used as source documents when creating sale orders. Let's say we create a quotation for our customer, Bike City, because they are interested in our new carbon wheelsets. They want to know if they can get a price break if they order a large quantity. The sales rep negotiates a discount with them and records it as a pricing condition in the quotation he/she creates. When the customer is ready to order, the sales rep simply creates the sales order using the CREATE WITH REFERENCE button, inputs the quotation number, and all the information from the quotation is copied into the sales order, including the negotiated price. The quotation is also saved in the document flow of the order so it can easily be found again. Any supporting paper documents or files can be scanned and attached to either the quotation or the sales order.

# 9 After the sale—returns and service

This chapter covers post-sales processes, including returns, service, and debit and credit memos.

## 9.1 Returns

Most businesses have to deal with returns, and Brand X is no exception. Standard SAP gives us the option to create returns with reference to the original customer invoice or sales order. At Brand X, our business process is to create the return order (order type CBFD) with reference to the invoice, because the invoice contains what was actually billed. All the information from the billing document is copied into the return order, and you have the option to select some or all of the items. A key point to note is that the pricing information is an exact copy of the information from the invoice, so we can be sure to refund the same amount that was paid. There are some industries where prices are very dynamic, and the process is to refund the current price back to the customer (as of the return date). In this case, the pricing date on the return order can be changed, and/or copy control settings can be configured to re-price, because documents are created 'with reference'.

Once saved, the return order number is given to the customer as the *RMA (return material authorization)* number. The RMA number is included with the returned product. When the returned item arrives at the warehouse, personnel look up that order number and create a *return delivery* from it. The return delivery is then used to record the items and quantities received, and once updated, a post goods receipt occurs. In our system, the post goods receipt of a return automatically moves the product into a special status to await quality inspection. Once the items are inspected, they can then be returned to regular inventory or to a used goods location.

After the items are received, billing is executed. In this case, because it is a return, a credit memo is created. In a credit memo, we do the opposite of a standard sale. The customer's A/R is credited, and revenue is debited. It's important to point out that because we use delivery-related billing here, we only credit the customer for the quantities and items received, which could be different from what was input into the return order (e.g., the customer says they are returning 10, but only 9 show up).

## 9.2    Credit and debit memo requests

Another special type of SAP sales document is the *credit memo request (CMR)* and its doppelganger, the *debit memo request (DMR)*. These sales orders are used to credit or debit a customer's account. For example, a customer didn't get their product on time, so we want to refund the freight charge from their purchase. We create a credit memo request, enter the customer number and a 'material' that represents the freight charge, enter a quantity and price, and then save. The material can be used to drive postings to specific G/L accounts as desired; in this example, it could be a freight account. When created, credit memo requests have a billing block automatically assigned. This means that a different person (usually in finance) can review the refund before releasing it, in order to ensure that no one gives the house away. CMRs and DMRs do not need a delivery, and billing occurs directly from the sales order.

## 9.3    Service and repairs

Companies that provide services have many options within the SAP system, from simple to more complex alternatives. For example, at Brand X one of our services is bike rental; we need to be able to rent a bike and collect payment for that rental. To support this, we have created a material called 'Bike Rental'. We use a material type called *service material (DIEN)*. By creating the material master with a service material type, the SAP system knows that this is different to a physical product. For example, there is no inventory or storage location needed for it. The service material type has a default item category group that determines the item category on the sales order. When we enter this material on the sales order, the item category is determined to indicate that this is a service line item. The configuration behind a service item category tells the system that no delivery document is necessary. We don't need to do an ATP check, and we don't need to pick, pack, and issue goods with such a service. All we need to do is price it and bill it. In a simple scenario like this, any costs related to the service provided are separate from it. Employees working with bike rentals could charge their time to a cost center or other cost object, and the same applies to any materials used.

On the other hand, many companies require a more granular view of service profitability, and need to manage the execution of more complex services. To achieve that, SAP has an entire module dedicated to services, called the *Customer Service (CS) module,* which is tightly integrated with Sales and

Distribution. We won't cover the CS module here, but we will look at two of the most tightly integrated scenarios relating to SD—repair orders and service order creation.

We already know that we can sell a product or service on standard sales orders, and we also know that it is the item category that informs the system at a line item level how to treat it. Let's now look at two additional services we offer at Brand X and how they are handled in the SAP system.

The first one is our 'MegaPack' system and installation. This is an offer to large bike stores that includes 100 bikes, and the setup and installation of a Brand X, three-tier display rack. To enable this in the SAP system, we have a material called 'MegaPack', which is a sales BOM. The sales BOM has eleven component materials—ten different types of bikes with a quantity of ten each, and an eleventh material called 'MegaInstall'. When the MegaPack material is entered into a sales order, it explodes out into eleven additional sales order lines. Based on configuration settings, the last line for the MegaInstall automatically triggers the creation of a *Service Order*. The service order, which is part of the CS module, is used to manage the execution of the installation. It contains the dates, people, and parts needed to complete and track the installation of a display rack at the bike store. It also collects all the costs related to the service, and ties them back to the sales order line item for item-level profitability, if desired.

The other scenario that is tightly integrated with SD is the in-house repair process. At Brand X, we make use of the standard SAP sales order type for repairs, not surprisingly called a *repair order*. The repair order gives us lots of flexibility in terms of defining our repair process; we can provide a bike on loan, or send a replacement, and we can offer a flat-rate price for the repair, or a price based on time and materials. The repair order helps us to manage typical questions that our customers and our business may have, such as: Has the bike been received back yet? Do we want to send a replacement bike instead? Has the customer been billed for the repairs? A key feature of repair orders is that they have an additional REPAIR tab on the header for both managing and tracking a repair (see Figure 9.1).

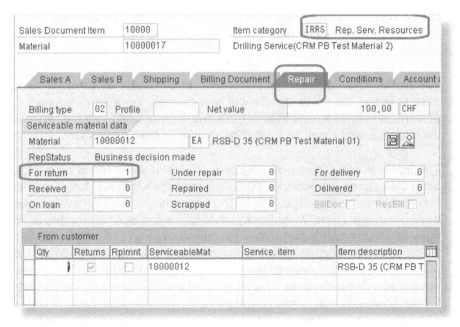

*Figure 9.1: Repair order*

On this tab, we can see a variety of fields that indicate the number of materials associated with each status: FOR RETURN, RECEIVED, ON LOAN, UNDER REPAIR, etc. In this example, we have one FOR RETURN item, meaning that we are expecting one item back from the customer. After we receive the item from the customer, the status automatically changes to one RECEIVED item. We then proceed to the next steps, such as UNDER REPAIR (i.e., a service order is created).

All this can be managed and tracked within the REPAIR tab. Behind the scenes, every input on the REPAIR tab triggers the creation of a new line on the sales order (this is hidden by default, but can be made visible if desired). Each one of these new lines triggers a follow-on action, which could be a line for the return delivery, a line for the loan item outbound delivery, a line to create the service order, a line for time and materials billing, etc.

# 10 Sales reporting

**In this chapter, we discuss the two types of sales reporting—transactional list reports and analytical reports.**

Lauren had finally reached the end of the order-to-cash process. She had created sales orders and deliveries, and picked, packed and shipped. She had executed post goods issue, billed, priced, and added text. After all that, she still had some questions: How does it all fit in with the day-to-day realities of running a business? How can you make sure everything is running smoothly, fix any problems that come up, and report on your results? She turned again to her trusty manual.

In general, we can break down our order-to-cash business process support into three main categories: executing business, managing the business flow, and analytical reporting. We've already seen a great deal about executing business. We know how to create sales orders, run the delivery due list, pick/pack/ship, and run a delivery due list. Now, it's time to take a look at reporting.

When it comes to managing the day-to-day business process flow, SAP provides a large number of apps to help move things along and keep a handle on what's happening. These are typically list reports that allow you to enter search criteria, generate document lists, and then take action, such as removing blocks.

Analytical reporting enables you to analyze data in flexible ways, in order to spot trends and track performance. In analytics, you can see how the business is doing against a certain metric (e.g., on-time orders), and then search for trends by examining the data by different criteria such as plant, customer group or material.

In earlier versions of SAP, analytical reporting took place in a separate reporting system, also known as Business Intelligence/Business Warehouse. Reporting was in a separate system, so the reports were not in real time. This was because it took time to transfer data from the transactional system (ECC) into the Business Intelligence system (BI). With the SAP S/4HANA platform, reporting and transactions have been integrated into one system, which allows for real-time reporting. What you see in the reports is an accurate and up-to-the-second reflection of what has occurred across the system. Additionally, with the revised architecture and lightning fast speed of

HANA, the time it takes to execute and process those reports is exponentially faster. When you then add the ability of Fiori to pull information from various transactions into one app, mash it up, and display that information on the tile itself, you've got a new and powerful approach to reporting. With each new release of SAP S/4HANA, more reporting apps are made available and the reporting catalog continues to grow.

As a general rule, you can divide reporting into *transactional list reports* and *analytical reports*. Transactional list reports help you to manage the day-to-day business of getting products out the door and orders billed. These reports provide information such as: a list of all blocked orders and the reasons they are blocked, a list of all shipping delays, and all the orders for a specific customer. Analytical reports enable you to analyze data for trends, and make it possible to 'slice and dice' the data in a variety of flexible ways. Analytical reports answer questions such as: What are our monthly sales? Who are our top customers? Which products are the most popular? Which geographical areas have good or bad sales results?

Lauren closed the manual and went back to her test system. She created a new Fiori group called 'Reporting' and added every sales reporting tile she could find into it (see Figure 10.1).

*Figure 10.1 : Sales reporting apps*

She tried the first one, LIST INCOMPLETE SALES DOCUMENTS, which seemed pretty straightforward. It listed sales orders that were missing something and needed to be fixed. It allowed her to sort the list by date and net value, so she could focus on fixing the biggest or oldest ones first (see Figure 10.2).

*Figure 10.2: Incomplete sales documents*

Returning to her reporting group, she clicked on the tile called SALES OR-DER FULFILMENT – ANALYZE ISSUES and a new report opened (see Figure 10.3).

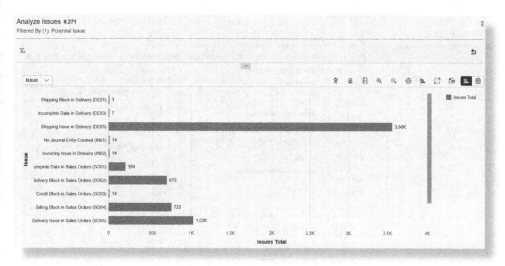

*Figure 10.3: Sales Order Fulfilment—issues display*

This one seemed like a full-fledged report. She could change the chart type from a bar graph to a line graph, or to a pie chart. She could filter and sort in a variety of different ways. From a business point of view, this looked like a good way to see and analyze what types of issues were impacting timely order fulfillment. This would be great for both managing day-to-day issues and getting an overview of trends. She also noticed that the incomplete sales orders list that she had seen in the previous app was included as one of the categories here.

Moving on, she launched the MY SALES OVERVIEW app (see Figure 10.4).

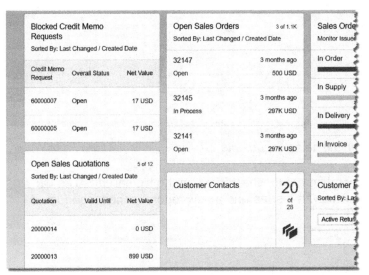

*Figure 10.4: My Sales Overview display*

She could see that this one was intended as a sort of landing page for sales managers. It looked a little bit like a sales cockpit, where she could see an overview of what was happening and what needed attention. The app included a series of embedded tiles, each with different sales information that she could drill into for more information. She saw that she could drag and drop the information cards (the different boxes) to where she wanted them.

In the MANAGE SALES ORDERS app, she saw that she could sort, select, and filter sales orders by a variety of criteria. She could then use that list to set or remove blocks, reject (cancel) orders, and even jump into creating sales orders (see Figure 10.5).

*Figure 10.5: Manage Sales Orders display*

She then looked at the reporting available from the ORDER-TO-CASH PER-FORMANCE – OVERVIEW tile. This looked like a great tool to get an overview of the order-to-cash information, in a cockpit format. She could drag the information cards to where she liked, and get a nice visual representation of the current status of orders, deliveries, and billing (see Figure 10.6).

*Figure 10.6: Order-to-Cash Performance Monitoring display*

Lauren then moved on to the SALES VOLUME – FLEXIBLE ANALYSIS tile. Here, she found a different category of reports which enabled her to analyze data in flexible ways. She could drag and drop fields into rows and columns, and create her own reports. They weren't something she would put in front of an end user, but they would be great for power users or more technical people.

Next, the DELIVERY PERFORMANCE app was also very helpful. It showed trend analyses and details about on-time delivery performance. From past experience, Lauren knew that this information was always of extreme interest to a variety of departments. It answered questions such as: Are we keeping our promises to our customers? When we say we will deliver something on a certain date, how are we tracking? It also offered the ability to see on-time performance by customer, and drill into sales orders to determine the root cause of an issue (see Figure 10.7).

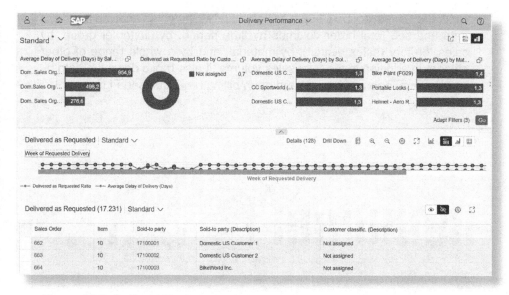

*Figure 10.7: Delivery Performance display*

Like all of the other reports, this one offered the ability to pick and choose which columns to show in the report. By clicking on the gear icon , she could bring up a VIEW SETTINGS screen in order to select the desired columns, and sort and group criteria (see Figure 10.8).

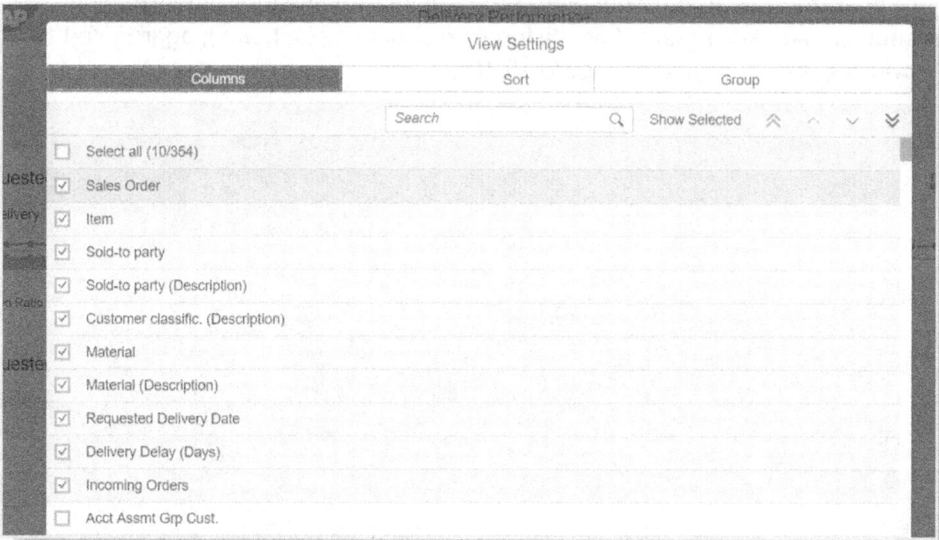

*Figure 10.8: Report settings*

Next, the SALES VOLUME app was very handy. She could analyze the sales data and see total order volumes by time period, by customer group, by sales territory (sales district), by material, and by a whole range of other criteria. In addition to the total sales volume, it also broke down the data by open orders, open deliveries, and open billing requests (see Figure 10.9).

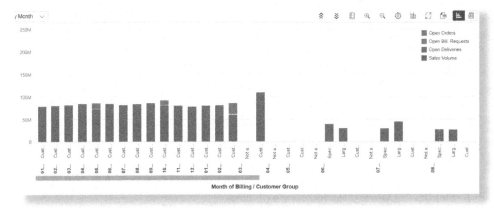

*Figure 10.9: Sales Volume app*

Lauren then took a look at the ORDER-TO-CASH PERFORMANCE – LAST 28 DAYS app. This analytical app enabled her to review performance across a number of pre-defined KPIs. She could display each of the KPIs in a variety of chart formats (bar, donut, line, etc.) against a variety of organizational structures (sales organization, distribution channel, plant, etc.), aggregated over the last 28 days (see Figure 10.10).

*Figure 10.10: Order-to-Cash Performance app—KPI definition*

The beauty of this app was that she could select which KPIs she wanted to track against, and save that as a report view. She also had heard that the company could define their own KPIs if none of the standard ones covered a desired statistic.

For a full definition of the key figures available in order-to-cash perform-ance, see the following link: *https://help.sap.com/doc/530c31553f2c9b5ae10 000000a44176d/1610%20002/en-US/frameset.htm?frameset.htm*

139

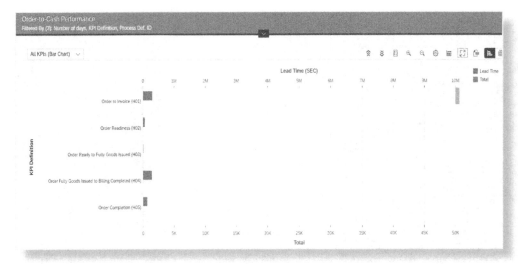

*Figure 10.11: Order-to-Cash Performance—Time Series app*

Next, Lauren explored the ORDER-TO-CASH PERFORMANCE – TIME SE-
RIES app. This analytical report gave her another view of KPIs, comparing
them against one another over time. It also provided the ability to create a
sequence of report views as an analysis path (see Figure 10.12).

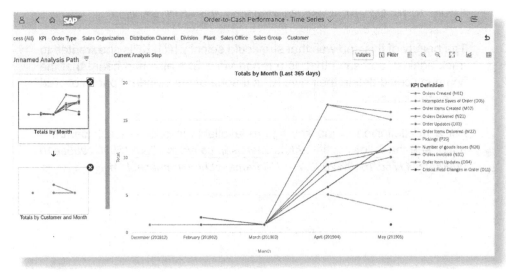

*Figure 10.12: Order-to-Cash Performance—Time Series display*

This could be useful for defining a series of reports in sequence, by first looking at one view of the data, and then at another. In the screenshot, we see a graphical representation of various KPIs over the last year—TOTALS BY MONTH (LAST 365 DAYS). We can then click on the next view, on the left, to see TOTALS BY CUSTOMER AND MONTH.

Rounding out the list of analytical apps, the SALES MANAGEMENT OVER-VIEW app offered Lauren another sales management cockpit view, this time with embedded sections that SAP calls cards, to help with day-to-day sales order management. Here, she saw that she could track orders and identify those that were blocked, overdue, or on backorder. She was also given a financial snapshot of order revenue and profit margin (see Figure 10.13).

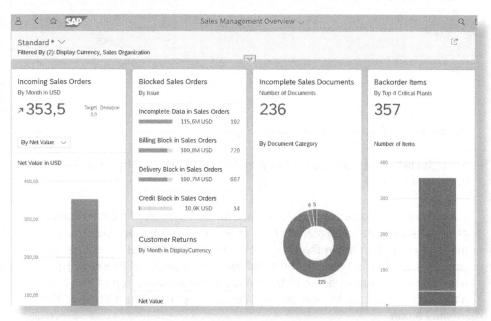

*Figure 10.13: Sales Management Overview display*

The last transactional list report that Lauren looked at was in the TRACK SALES ORDERS app. This report provided a quick way to find particular sales orders, to see all the orders for a particular customer, or to view all the orders in a certain status (see Figure 10.14).

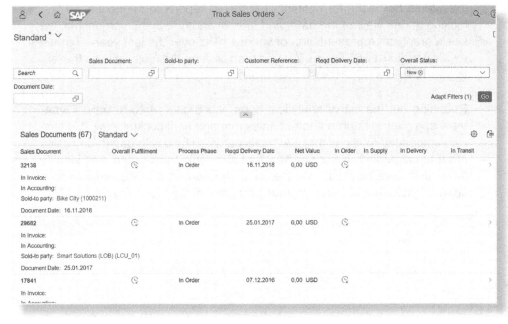

*Figure 10.14: Track Sales Orders display*

From the list, she could quickly drill into the particular order by selecting the document number.

Lauren was impressed with what she had seen. There were a large number of standard reports available. With a little more exploration, she realized that she could trim down the list to come up with a key set of reports that would enable her to optimize the order-to-cash business at Brand X. However, she wondered what the options were if she wanted a report that wasn't already delivered as part of the standard reports? She turned to her manual again.

## 10.3.1 Custom reporting

The SAP S/4 release has provided new tools which allow super users to build their own custom reports. Lauren discovered the QUERY BROWSER app, which has a large catalog of *CDS (core data services) views* (a logically joined set of tables), from which users can build their own reports (see Figure 10.15).

142

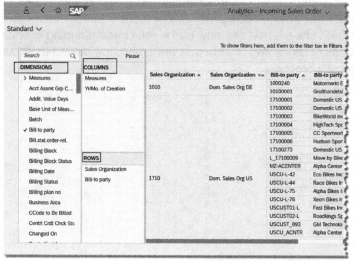

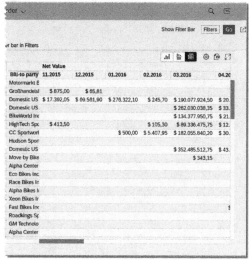

*Figure 10.15: Report builder*

The screenshot shows a report being built based on the INCOMING SALES ORDER CDS view (C_SALESORDERITEMQRY). All of the fields available in this view are presented, and various reporting DIMENSIONS can be dragged and dropped to the COLUMNS and ROWS sections, instantly adding them to the report. Next, filtering and sorting preferences can be added. Then, best of all, the newly created report is saved as a tile which can be shared with target users.

Lauren closed the manual and slowly exhaled. She had covered a lot of ground these last few days. Although she knew there was still much more to learn about SAP, she felt that she now had a solid understanding of what the various pieces of Sales and Distribution were, and how they fit together in the order-to-cash process.

# 11 Summary

You did it! Like Lauren, you've now completed your first steps in SAP SD!

You learned what a module is and explored the overall SAP solution. You covered the order-to-cash process and the key flow from sales order to delivery to billing document. You explored the function of the enterprise structure, and learned about the concept of master data and the key master data objects in sales: business partners, materials, and pricing. You dove into the foundational document—the sales order—and learned about its structure, with a header, line items, and schedule lines. You looked at output and deliveries and billing. You joined Lauren on her journey as she started at her new company and got up to speed with a real live SAP system. Along the way, you had many lessons in 'SAPanese'—the wild and woolly world of SAP acronyms and terminology. Finally, you looked at the many options available in sales reporting. You even learned that an IDoc isn't an ophthalmologist!

Having completed this voyage of discovery, you should now be well equipped to navigate your way through the SAP SD module!

 **ESPRESSO TUTORIALS**

**You have finished the book.**

# A The Author

John von Aspen is a business technology expert with over 23 years' experience with SAP products and implementation projects. John started his career with SAP America, where he served for ten years before launching his own independent consulting business. His areas of expertise in SAP include the Order-to-Cash business processes, Sales and Distribution (SD), Customer Service (CS), Enterprise Asset Management (EAM), E-Commerce, and Digital Payments.

# B Index

# C Disclaimer

This publication contains references to the products of SAP SE.

SAP, R/3, SAP NetWeaver, Duet, PartnerEdge, ByDesign, SAP Business-Objects Explorer, StreamWork, and other SAP products and services mentioned herein as well as their respective logos are trademarks or registered trademarks of SAP SE in Germany and other countries.

Business Objects and the Business Objects logo, BusinessObjects, Crystal Reports, Crystal Decisions, Web Intelligence, Xcelsius, and other Business Objects products and services mentioned herein as well as their respective logos are trademarks or registered trademarks of Business Objects Software Ltd. Business Objects is an SAP company.

Sybase and Adaptive Server, iAnywhere, Sybase 365, SQL Anywhere, and other Sybase products and services mentioned herein as well as their respective logos are trademarks or registered trademarks of Sybase, Inc. Sybase is an SAP company.

SAP SE is neither the author nor the publisher of this publication and is not responsible for its content. SAP Group shall not be liable for errors or omissions with respect to the materials. The only warranties for SAP Group products and services are those that are set forth in the express warranty statements accompanying such products and services, if any. Nothing herein should be construed as constituting an additional warranty.

# More Espresso Tutorials Books

Kevin Riddell, Rajen Iyver:

## Practical Guide to SAP® GTS, Part 1: SPL Screening and Compliance Management

▶ Tips and tricks for leveraging SAP GTS to automate trade compliance

▶ Walk step by step through business processes

▶ Overview of regulatory requirements and compliance suggestions

▶ Review of Version 11.0 with screenshots

*http://5100.espresso-tutorials.com*

Kevin Riddell, Rajen Iyver:

## Practical Guide to SAP® GTS, Part 2: Preference and Customs Management

▶ Best practices for leveraging SAP GTS for trade compliance

▶ Fundamentals of preference implementation and system set up

▶ How self-filing, broker models and free trade agreements can improve ROI

▶ Review of Version 11.0 with screenshots

*http://5134.espresso-tutorials.com*

Tobias Götz, Anette Götz:

**Practical Guide to SAP® Transportation Management (2nd edition)**

▶ Supported business processes

▶ Best practices

▶ Integration aspects and architecture

▶ Comparison and differentiation to similar SAP components

*http://5082.espresso-tutorials.com*

Kevin Riddell, Rajen Iyver:

**Practical Guide to SAP® GTS, Part 3: Bonded Warehouse, Foreign Trade Zone, and Duty Drawback**

▶ Leveraging and configuring bonded warehouse

▶ Fundamentals of foreign trade zones

▶ How business users can get the most out of GTS functionality

▶ Detailed configuration and user guides for bonded warehouse and foreign trade zones

*http://5162.espresso-tutorials.com*

Marjorie Wright:

## Credit Management in SAP® S/4HANA

▶ Basic configuration settings
▶ Integration points with FI-AR and SD
▶ Organizational structure and master data
▶ Business Partner master record

*http://5300.espresso-tutorials.com*

Made in United States
North Haven, CT
06 May 2022

18971298R00085